LEADER LEVITY AND THE POWER OF BAKED ALASKA

Simple ways to lead people and build business

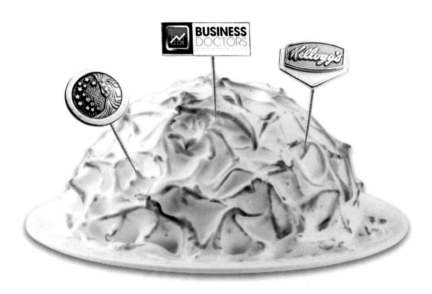

STEVEN J. SMITH

Leadership, Levity and the Power of Baked Alaska
Simple ways to lead people and build business

Copyright © 2021 Steven J. Smith

Business / Leadership

Printed in the United Kingdom

ISBN 978-1-5272-9297-0

Published by Higher Plane Consulting Ltd

Editorial Production: The Editor's Chair

To Donna,

One of the pleasures of the last eighteen months of lockdowns has been meeting wonderful people like you!

Matthew Chapter Five, Verse Thirteen:

'Ye are the salt of the earth'.

1. A person or group considered as embodying simplicity and moral integrity.

2. Archaic. A person or group considered the best or most worthy part of society.

Salt of the earth—*The Free Dictionary*

Best regards,

Steve

TITHE

A tithe is a one-tenth part of something paid as a contribution to a religious organisation or compulsory tax to government. In this instance, I am tithing the net sales revenue that I receive to distribute among ten national and local charities relevant to the events shared in this book.

Grocery Aid

Group B Strep Support

Liverpool Heart and Chest Hospital

Prince and Princess of Wales Hospice, Glasgow

Standing Tall Foundation

Stroke Information

The Lewy Body Society

The Steve Prescott Foundation

Wigan Youth Zone

Willowbrook Hospice, St Helens

THEMES

FOREWORD

When I met Steve, our relationship was one in which I was his career coach.

After he invited me to review his book and pen a foreword, I readily agreed to do so. My fifty-year career in human resource (HR) management and associated HR activities qualified me to comment on peoples' personal qualities, professional skills and career experience… the three things at the heart of Steve's book.

When we first talked, I was struck by Steve's energy, commitment, and capacity to be self-effacing: a characteristic in ample supply throughout this uniquely informative and entertaining romp through his career.

He draws on his personal career experiences with acute honesty and provides a plethora of anecdotes on leadership, sales, promotions and their resulting successes and failures; all of which make this book a most unusual and welcome contribution to the crowded (some would say, overcrowded) market for business books.

Steve admits to having had as many downs as ups, but through it all comes bright lights of wisdom and humour, in equal measure.

I heartily recommend *Baked Alaska*, especially for those of us who have grown weary of the over full bookshelves of self-important tomes! This is the authentic, real deal.

Colin Parry OBE, JP, FCIPD

CHRONOLOGY

1968	Born in St. Helens
1973-85	Nutgrove Primary, Grange Park High School
1985-87	Widnes Sixth Form College
1987-90	University of Sheffield
1990-99	Procter & Gamble
1999-04	The Kellogg Company
2004-19	AG Barr plc
2019	Flavour Warehouse Limited
2020	Business Doctor for St. Helens, Wigan, Widnes & Leigh
2021	Baked Alaska

KEY TERMS

Blue-chip - Companies with stable and strong financial track records based on continuous success

Brand - Product manufactured by a particular company, under a particular name

CEO - Chief Executive Officer

Consumers - The end users of a product

Customers - The purchaser of products, usually a wholesaler or retailer for onward selling

FMCG - Fast moving consumer goods

HBR - Harvard Business Review

HR - Human Resources (Personnel)

MD - Managing Director

Multiples - National grocery retail chains who buy direct from suppliers (e.g., Asda, Co-operative, Tesco)

NPD - New Product Development

PA - Personal Assistant

PLC - Public Limited Company

Shopper - The person who buys the product in-store but may not be the actual consumer of it

SKU - Shelf (or Stock) Keeping Unit (e.g., a five-hundred-gram packet of Kellogg Cornflakes is one SKU)

SME - Small to Medium-sized Enterprise

Wholesalers - 'Middlemen' who buy in bulk from suppliers and sell to small retailers (e.g., Booker)

USP - Unique Selling Proposition of a product

SCENE SETTING

FMCG or consumer packaged goods are products that are sold quickly at a relatively low cost. Examples include non-durable household goods such as packaged foods, beverages, toiletries, over-the-counter medicines and other consumable products. Wholesalers, supermarkets and convenience stores sell these products in their millions every day and they are a core part of life as we know it.

We can take these everyday products for granted—until something like a pandemic comes along and makes us realise how valuable toilet paper and hand sanitisers are to us. I see a correlation between our approach to these simple items and the simple workplace scenarios we often overlook that could teach us plenty, if only we paid closer attention. That's what I have tried to do in this book.

I have had a thirty-year career in marketing and selling everyday items— from Fairy Liquid to Frosties—primarily to supermarkets, working with great companies and well-known brands. This book sets out to share parts of my experiences and learning that I hope will be of interest and value to others, revealing simple ways to develop leadership and performance. The building of trust and respect helps everyone to perform better and feel happier in their work. Some basic observations and interventions can add up to marginal and even significant gains.

Commentary and guidance on leadership, management and analysis of the skills and competencies required to succeed in business have been published and will continue to be published over again. John Adair and Simon Sinek instantly come to my mind and if you want to understand the thoughts and philosophies of successful and revered business minds, seek out any number of books about Jack Welch, Steve Jobs or Bill Gates. Maybe even Donald Trump? Or maybe not! On the UK side of the Atlantic, take your pick from James Dyson, Alan Sugar or Allan Leighton, for example. There are thousands of biographies and autobiographies of the many visionaries, leaders of corporations and the consultants, commentators and academics who have studied them.

I have taken a different and slightly more irreverent approach. This is not to denigrate industries, organisations or individuals who have facilitated the supply of life's essentials but to try to share learning and insights in an easy-to-digest format. Similar to Jim Rohn and Chris Wideners' classic short story *Twelve Pillars*, *Baked Alaska* is an easy read for personal development.

Peter Kay has developed a phenomenally successful comedy career and a place in the nation's heart often by just highlighting mundane events in a comedic light. There is much more to Peter's talent of course, but these are some of the building blocks of his humour. His *Car Share* TV series was a hilarious portrayal of a superstore manager providing a checkout operator with a daily lift to work, musing on everyday occurrences. Quite apt as you read through this book.

So, carry on for 'warts and all' observations from someone who has worked closely with many great and not-so-great business leaders. I have enjoyed my career and believe I have earned widespread respect, meaning I can be frank and light-hearted as I meander through my career memories.

I won't share many names as the purpose is neither to laud organisational 'heroes' nor score points off those caught out when they were still learning. However, I can assure readers that the situations and scenarios described were all observed by me or passed on from reliable and trusted sources. There are a few 'myths' and 'legends' (concerning glove puppets for example), that would be difficult for me to substantiate, though the stories at the time were quite well articulated across the grocery trade. I may end up losing some acquaintances along the way if they recognise where I have referred to their actions in a poor light and

I am not shy of acknowledging my own mistakes either. There are some valuable lessons from telling this story, so it is worth the risk. As the saying goes: 'You can't make an omelette without cracking a few eggs'.

The fundamental lesson is how to get the best out of the people you work for, work with and those you manage yourself. Countless theoretical tomes have been produced on people management, coaching others and personal development. Hours and hours of research, profiles and models have been developed to help you understand yourself, your team, and the colleagues around you. Many organisations will determine where you are on the Insights Wheel or how you are profiled through Myers-Briggs. Different companies and managers place varying levels of importance on this type of analysis and some development tools are more useful than others. Ultimately, I would suggest that developing people is not hard. Really, with a modicum of common sense and courtesy, it just isn't that difficult.

In business, we also invariably encounter situations that are not binary. There are circumstances where simple yes/no decisions (with nothing in between) are required, but even matters of law or regulation can still be open to interpretation. Decisions are often based on judgement or intuition and things are rarely black or white. I have always referred to this as *playing in the grey zone*. I am not referring to 'sitting on the fence', 'hedging your bets' or procrastination, more to a situation where there just aren't clear right or wrong outcomes. I have seen some people struggle with this concept whilst others leverage it to the advantage of their business and themselves. One of the 'Beliefs of Excellence' I was introduced to by Cecara Consulting was that 'everyone makes the best possible choice available to them at the time'.

Another of the 'Beliefs of Excellence' is 'the person with the most flexibility in thinking and behaviour stands the best chance of success'. On that basis, a lot of what I have written are *my* views and *my* interpretation of situations. Readers can judge my take on events for themselves, as, although I have quoted Matthew 5:13, my views aren't to be taken as gospel.

I aim to provoke thought, inspire action and hopefully provide a little levity and amusement along the way. Eager readers can learn much more from the follow-up study of the theories and disciplines referenced and alluded to. The *Harvard Business Review* is also a fine source of revelatory thinking that has influenced my perspective in several fields.

You will notice quite a few sporting references and analogies as you read through. I apologise to those who have no interest in football (soccer) or rugby and hope they stick with the book anyway. Watching live sport has been a key part of my life and whilst I know that many find it boring, there are often similarities between sport and business, particularly in the areas of teamwork, motivation and performance.

I applied for a position as an independent non-executive director for the Professional Footballers Association in 2020. Unfortunately, I wasn't successful, but aside from the remuneration, my key motivation was a firm belief in the positive power that football can exert in society and a desire to help channel this. Most newspaper and media coverage of professional footballers tend to be about their excesses and bling lifestyles. However, look at what Marcus Rashford achieved in changing UK government policy for the benefit of disadvantaged kids. Consider the joy and love that Jermaine Defoe brought into the tragically short life of little Bradley Lowery. Also, Neville Southall has become a social justice campaigner using Twitter to highlight vulnerability and champion issues affecting many who are overlooked in society. Top sports stars often have the potential for greater positive influence than politics, religion, or the corporate social responsibility policies of large companies.

To summarise sections, I have captured *my* key thoughts and insights as simple (car) bumper stickers to ponder on. Easily digested and remembered.

Baked Alaska can't promise to divulge secrets on how to 'double your business overnight', 'guarantee step changes in performance' or 'supercharge your career progression', but it will provide honest, down-to-earth advice on how to treat people appropriately, gain their trust and respect and learn from my mistakes (and successes of course!).

Gary Vaynerchuk, chairman of Vayner X, captured similar sentiments when saying, 'I'm not here to give "advice", I'm here sharing experiences and observations from my life/career with the most context and clarity and consistency that I can. I'm hopeful that people take the map and build on it and use it. I'm here trying to "win", but the trophies I'm chasing and how I go about getting them are different—I think it can help a lot of people be happier if they chase what matters to them.'

I completed this work in 2020, a quite unprecedented year since the Coronavirus disrupted life as we knew it. To highlight one key positive would be the resilience shown by people across the globe. That isn't to ignore the sadness and despair, but rather to celebrate the individual, community and business resilience that came to the fore. I read a forbes.com article explaining 'Why the word for 2021 is resilience' and I completely agree.

A. LEADING PEOPLE:
THE GOOD, THE BAD AND THE UGLY

CHAPTER 1

BAD MANNERS

Emotional Intelligence

A standard definition of emotional intelligence is 'the ability to identify and manage one's own emotions, as well as the emotions of others'. It is generally viewed as comprising three skills:

1) emotional awareness or the ability to identify one's own emotions

2) the ability to harness those emotions and apply them to tasks like thinking and problem solving

3) the ability to manage emotions, which includes regulating one's own emotions and helping others to do the same

Awareness of peoples' intelligence quotient (IQ) is a generally familiar concept, whereas an understanding of emotional quotient (EQ) is less well known. The importance of EQ in business has been studied and analysed comprehensively by a multitude of others, so I am going to share thoughts and observations on a basic level.

I can always remember my grandmother saying that there was 'no shame in being poor, but soap and water don't cost much, and good manners don't cost anything'. Developing that simple concept, there can be a lot to admire in someone who is fiercely committed, incredibly driven and highly successful, but it only takes a few seconds to thank others and some seldom do.

Early in my career, perhaps naively, I was quite shocked at conferences and meetings where you could be engaged in conversation with someone who would 'cut you dead' and abruptly terminate the discussion because they'd spotted an opportunity to talk to someone far more senior and influential. I have experienced people turning their back and moving off mid-sentence on many occasions. It took me a while to understand what was happening and who the worst culprits were. Not only is this incredibly rude, but of course it's very short-term thinking. There is a good chance that your paths will continue to cross, and people may need your help, support, or input in the future. You may one day become more senior to them or even become their direct manager. There is a saying that you 'reap what you sow' and some people's short-sightedness means they often plant bad seeds or sometimes sow none at all.

Courtesy

It also never ceases to amaze me how in business, some people leave their manners at home when they head into work. People from all manner of backgrounds. For some, it can appear like they are two people. Someone who is affable outside of work can seem to operate like a 'bastard' at their desk. *Good morning*, *please* and *thank you* are often in short supply.

Contrast that type of behaviour to that of David Stirling, founder of the Special Air Service (SAS), renowned as the toughest of all the world's military special forces. In *SAS: Rogue Heroes the Authorised Wartime History,* author Ben MacIntyre described Stirling as 'exquisitely polite to all' and said that he 'did not bark orders; he asked people to do things'.

I am sure the friends and relatives of some colleagues I have encountered would be horrified if shown how they have treated others in the workplace. From lack of courtesy and rudeness through to premeditated political and exploitative behaviour.

It may well be that some of these behaviours are intended to cover personal inadequacy or some deep-rooted insecurity. Of course, there can also be a backdrop of genuine psychological conditions, such as anxiety or autism where someone may not be able to appreciate the impact of how they interact with others. However, many unfortunately choose to behave in these ways and still make it to the higher reaches of organisations. On occasion they will then go on to stress the importance of emotional intelligence in leadership after high- level executive coaching, a Ted Talk or reading an article, despite having rarely exhibited any EQ themselves.

I've always been understanding and perhaps the lack of a more cynical edge has held me back, though there are many highly qualified proponents of 'Servant' or 'Alpha Leadership' models (Ken Blanchard captures this superbly) which are adamant that this is not the way to succeed in the modern world. Courtesy and consideration of others are not expensive in terms of time or money.

I recently spotted a great post on LinkedIn by The Female Lead, stating that character is how you treat those who can do nothing for you. Spot on!

Internal Affairs

Consider this scenario; someone has just been appointed to a senior leadership role heading a large team. Many are wary of them due to their perceived aggressive style in the past. Business is not currently great, and morale is dipping. When arriving each morning, how would you expect them to behave?

a) Stride into the building as normal, avoiding eye contact, enter their office and close the door without acknowledging anyone else.

b) Mutter a few *hellos* with their head down as they walk along to their office, then close the door and have their back to everyone as they log on.

c) Stroll in a little more casually, greet the people who are already at their desks with a bright 'good morning' and engage a few in brief but pertinent conversation.

I have seen someone stick rigidly to option a) until external performance coaches suggested that b) or ideally c) would lift morale and help the individual connect with their team. Extremely basic advice that did not come cheap!

I have also witnessed individuals in quite senior positions be rude, aggressive, and overly challenging to just about everyone around them and particularly derogatory to the most junior or lower grade members of staff. You can argue that in a meeting with peers, all should be able to stick up for themselves, but it rarely helps effective teamwork if one person is always going to be objectionable and difficult.

Here is another scenario.

An MD has an extremely sensitive announcement to release that will be distressing for many employees. As the MD, after releasing the announcement, would you...?

a) Stay in your own office at headquarters and block out your diary.

b) Be a visible and reassuring presence but encourage business as usual.

c) 'Drag race' your new Ferrari down the car park when you leave early, causing people to rise from their desks to see what the noise is.

If you would take approach a), isn't that lacking in courage and good manners? If the answer is c), is that because you'd be completely oblivious to the impact on others, unaware of how insensitive your actions might be, or you just don't care? You need a thick skin at times in management, perhaps even thicker the higher you get, but surely actions like c) are completely unnecessary and potentially very damaging. Unfortunately, ill-considered behaviour like this does happen.

I was once in a planning meeting where someone shared an idea that was immediately described by a senior person as the stupidest idea they'd ever heard. It became a standing joke for the individual who fortunately took it in good heart and attributed it to the eccentricity of the person saying it. Ironically, his idea was later used by the business on multiple occasions.

I am acutely aware of many of my mistakes and not afraid to highlight them. I once briefed someone on a proposed structural change just before the team meeting that they were about to lead. By relieving them of some pressure and promoting someone they had coached and developed I anticipated the proposal to be received positively. It wasn't! They interpreted it as a dilution of their role and responsibilities, which had made it very challenging for them to keep up a positive appearance through the meeting.

On another occasion, I was considering internal and external candidates for a role. Once I had made my decision, I was so focused on getting on with things that I neglected to inform the internal candidate directly that they had been unsuccessful. They found out from my public announcement about the new person coming in. This rude oversight was quite rightly highlighted to me by a colleague. Obviously, I apologised to the person concerned immediately, but this was incredibly poor form on my part. Fortunately, the person was understanding and knew it was out of character.

Anyone can make mistakes or errors of judgement. The most important aspect is to recognise, apologise, learn from them and not repeat. In the first scenario mentioned earlier, a manager returning to the unengaging behaviour once morale had improved would demonstrate a lack of sincerity. In the second scenario, arranging a Bentley test drive at the office, on the day of another serious announcement would be pretty crass from my perspective!

The Sales Interface

Looking at supplier and customer relationships, things have changed quite dramatically. When I started, it was typically the main blue-chip manufacturing companies that toured university milk rounds (career fairs effectively). They would compete to hire the 'cream of the graduate crop' and those who had studied but weren't necessarily committed to a vocational or professional career path.

In the retail and wholesale sectors, there were a lot of people who had worked their way up through their organisations, developing their skills on the job and working in stores as opposed to on campus. At times, this created tension as 'canny' buyers would seek to put down 'cocky' graduates from suppliers. I even heard stories of physical altercations though it never happened to me. I was shouted at, insulted and on one occasion even threatened in a message left on my home answerphone by a store manager who had not received his stock. Some managers appeared to view their stores as their own petty fiefdom and a lot of inexperienced salespeople did not have the interpersonal skills to deal with this kind of behaviour.

In one of my first ever sales meetings I turned up with my Procter & Gamble trainer to meet the senior buyer at a cash and carry. None of us had met before and when my trainer explained that I would be the account manager going forward, the buyer was quite angry. He complained that he had constantly changing Procter & Gamble contacts who were 'wet behind the ears', didn't understand his business and once they had learned were swiftly moved on, replaced by another and the cycle started again. I knew I needed to learn quickly and get things right. A year later when I was promoted to a new role, he apologised for the initial hard time, thanked me for all I had done and wished me well. I have always cherished this acknowledgement. He had the guts and decency to apologise. At times humility is an only too rare commodity.

John Baines is now a very well-respected elder statesman in the UK wholesale sector. I like him a lot and we still reminisce about his warm and friendly welcome.

Another of my first responsibilities on joining Procter & Gamble was to manage the Batleys' cash & carry near Liverpool. The buyer there, Mr Jones, was a burly and belligerent chap renowned amongst sales reps for his dislike of graduates. I got on well with the other staff in the depot and one of the young lads who worked in the warehouse used to try to wind me up before my meetings by shouting 'Big bad Jones, breaks rep's bones'. I did my best to get on with the buyer and ensure I provided the best possible service, but I was a tad nervous when my district manager was coming to work with me for the day and Batleys was a scheduled visit. A brief meeting with the buyer was littered with the f-word and various other expletives, although I did complete my meeting objectives. We then had the obligatory debrief in the car and fearing the worst I apologised for how the buyer had behaved. I was quite taken aback when he laughed and said that I'd 'performed well', had 'won the buyer over' and developed a good relationship—'believe me, he wouldn't have behaved like that if he didn't like you'.

The district manager reflected those sentiments as he advised me of my first step up the Procter & Gamble ladder whilst we were sat in a

McDonalds in Liverpool a few months later. Fantastic news for me, albeit not in a particularly glamourous setting. To be fair though, several years later when I was advised of promotion to sales controller level, my then boss ordered a bottle of champagne as we sat outside Ruthin Castle on a balmy summer's evening—that was more like it!

Over time the playing field of course levelled. The grocery multiples made key appointments from within their blue-chip supplier base (for example, Allan Leighton at Asda was ex-Mars) and competed for the top graduates to run their stores and manage head office functions, particularly buying and marketing. Over thirty years I have enjoyed some wonderful productive relationships with customer contacts, working with incredibly talented people, many of whom continue to climb the career ladder—fundamentally decent people with whom it has been a pleasure to do business.

Of course, I've also encountered rude and overly aggressive types with little respect for the people with whom they interact. Constantly applying excessive pressure and effectively bullying suppliers does not make anyone a better person, nor elevate them to any kind of special status. It is unnecessary and archaic behaviour.

A few points to ponder

- **In plain and simple terms, people do not respond well to rudeness, being treated like crap or being looked down on.**

- **Disagreement and conflict will always occur—you must find a way to deal with them productively.**

- **People 'click' with some more than others and great results can follow.**

- **However, even when you are not someone's greatest fan, discourtesy achieves little.**

- **You reap what you sow.**

- **A touch of humility has a powerful effect.**

- **Character is how you treat those who can do nothing for you.**

CHAPTER 2

E IS FOR LEADERSHIP

The great philosophical question I first encountered at university is, 'Are leaders born or made?' This has been examined deeply, like David Rooke and William Torbert in the *HBR* who suggest that leaders are made, not born. From my perspective, like most things in life, the truth probably lies somewhere between them. Some show innate leadership qualities at an early age whilst others talk of voyages of development where leaders can change substantially. For me, the answer is not black or white, it is in the grey zone.

Most businesses, and particularly those in the FMCG industry, place great emphasis on leadership in the way they recruit and develop the people they believe will one day lead their organisations to ongoing success and profit growth. The concept of leadership is introduced to children in the playground through games like 'Follow My Leader' and the introduction of form captains and Head Girl/Boy as their education develops. You could spend the rest of your life trawling through online material about leadership. I found a piece on taskque.com highlighting no less than fifteen traits that make great leaders (and you could still add to this list):

1. Honesty and integrity
2. Confidence
3. Inspiring others
4. Commitment and passion
5. Good communicator
6. Decision-making capabilities

7. Accountability
8. Delegation and empowerment
9. Creativity and innovation
10. Empathy
11. Resilience
12. Emotional intelligence
13. Humility
14. Transparency
15. Vision and purpose

Glenn Leibowitz shared his thirteen traits of exceptional leaders and I loved the way he employed plain, straightforward English. This makes them that little bit more down-to-earth and accessible.

1. They trust you to do the job you've been hired to do.
2. They seek your advice and input.
3. They find opportunities to let you shine.
4. They recognise your contributions.
5. They have your back during tough times.
6. They are master storytellers.
7. They challenge you to do bigger and better things.
8. They express appreciation.
9. They are responsive.
10. They know when to apologise.
11. They give credit where credit is due.
12. They treat others with dignity and respect.
13. They care.

You could bankrupt yourself by buying all the books on this subject. I've read a few, such as *Effective Leadership* by John Adair, and Allan Leighton compiled *On Leadership* by talking to dozens of successful business leaders. My preference is to highlight ideas and let readers work out for themselves how to develop their own leadership style.

When interviewing prospective sales managers, I often used to ask candidates to define the words leadership and strategy. Whilst stressing that there were no definitive answers, it was always interesting to observe such a diverse range of understanding for words featuring so prominently in business.

The 3E Model

Procter & Gamble introduced me to the 3E model of leadership representing:

- Envisioning
- Enabling
- Energising

Envisioning:

Taking an idea and making it into a plan. Clarifying the concept, making it real and mapping out the steps to achieve it. Ensuring consistency of understanding, clarity of expectations and appreciation of priorities.

Enabling:

Providing tools and support materials. Ensuring the appropriate knowledge and technology is available as required. Coaching and developing the skills needed. Delivering an appropriate environment to facilitate success.

Energising:

Ensuring everyone is 'up for it' by creating the right culture and ensuring role models and managers' behaviours are consistent. Infusing others with drive, determination, and enthusiasm.

This is the model I have invariably referenced throughout my career although many other frameworks incorporate the letter E. Procter & Gamble's 3Es can be expanded to five by adding Enrol and Execute. London Business School has a 5E model which consists of:

- Envision
- Express
- Excite
- Enable
- Execute

And you could add a whole host of other words starting with E such as Equip, Empower, Encourage, Edge, Effective, Emotive, Efficient, Explain, Effervesce… Okay, so it is easy to get carried away, but as a mental exercise readers can see how many other words beginning with E they could use in a leadership model—I have provided another one in this sentence!

The Cost of Poor Leadership

Gina Gardiner, leading author and key proponent of enlightened leadership, and CEO of Genuinely You Ltd, highlights the impact of poor leadership from a personal, business and societal perspective. It is quite staggering—the cost of lost productivity and efficiency due to absenteeism alone is estimated at over seventy billion pounds in the UK.

It isn't that much of a surprise anymore when people get to senior positions and demonstrate poor leadership skills, poor judgement and a complete lack of appreciation for how they treat others.

The Dominic Cummings Barnard Castle 'eye test' affair during the first UK lockdown immediately springs to mind when he broke the rules on travel. I also shared a hard-hitting article on LinkedIn that I read about in *Sports Illustrated* in the wake of Greg Clarke's resignation as Football Association Chairman in November 2020. It was pretty scathing, but I agreed with the sentiment:

'At a time when football desperately needed leadership, Clarke has been a disgrace. He lacked the subtlety to play political games, allowed himself to drift on the tides of tabloid opinion and was devoid of any moral authority. That in little more than an hour he was able to bumble through a checklist of almost every outmoded stereotype before a parliamentary committee was only the final straw.'

Dark Triad Leadership

The concept of dark triad leadership was introduced on a coaching session I attended run by Professor Vicky Vass from the InTouch network. It is pretty scary stuff. I highlight many examples of damaging 'leadership' behaviours throughout the book and know from experience that those who practice them often still flourish and progress in organisations.

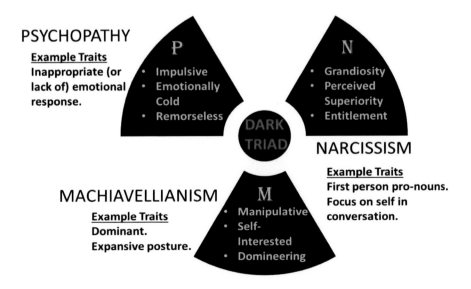

PSYCHOPATHY

Example Traits
Inappropriate (or lack of) emotional response.

P
- Impulsive
- Emotionally Cold
- Remorseless

DARK TRIAD

N
- Grandiosity
- Perceived Superiority
- Entitlement

NARCISSISM

Example Traits
First person pro-nouns. Focus on self in conversation.

MACHIAVELLIANISM

Example Traits
Dominant.
Expansive posture.

M
- Manipulative
- Self-Interested
- Domineering

I am not suggesting that anyone I've worked with was the British equivalent of Patrick Bateman (from the film *American Psycho*), but I have witnessed some of his traits!

A few points to ponder

- **Leaders are born *and* made!**

- **Leadership opportunities can come early.**

- **Speaking in plain English enables everyone.**

- **You cannot climb the leadership ladder without the letter E!**

- **Leaders require the capacity to inspire, a strong sense of purpose and social responsibility and to lead through care and compassion, not fear and blame.**

CHAPTER 3

POWER TO THE PEOPLE

The Best Possible Start

Way back in 1919, William Cooper Procter continued a series of efforts to create the strongest of bonds between the Procter & Gamble company and its employees by revising the articles of incorporation to identify that 'the interests of the company and its employees are inseparable'. This commitment to people certainly continued through to my joining, which meant it was a fantastic environment to start one's career in. Developing people was always at the forefront and the initial training was first class. I still use skills and concepts Procter & Gamble introduced me to going way back to the reading materials sent before I'd even started!

There is a long list of Procter & Gamble alumni who have gone on to significant leadership roles across the globe. For example, Paul Polman was UK MD for a spell in the nineties and eventually became CEO of arch-rivals Unilever. This is of course testament to the skills and abilities of individuals, not just the training and support they receive. Jim Stengel captured this at an alumni gathering in the US when he said that 'Joining P&G is like joining an elite group of leaders. It's a very intense experience that stays with you long after you leave the company. Like athletic teams, P&G binds people together for their entire life.'

Training

I have sat through hours and hours of training programmes during my career and a few things stand out. Firstly, the number of times I have seen similar materials (usually originating at Procter & Gamble, Mars or Unilever) adapted, developed and re-presented by others.

Secondly, I have occasionally participated with genuine awe and admiration of presenters and coaches who have shared thought-provoking concepts and ideas. At Kellogg's, the sales director brought in a company called Cecara. Their ideas were really forward-thinking, and their Beliefs of Excellence have continually influenced my view of the world. I've also at times looked on incredulously thinking 'how on earth can this person be making a living from this?' As with many situations, there is the good, the bad, the average and sometimes the incredulous.

There is a saying that 'those who can, do and those who can't, teach' but to be fair, I've witnessed people that I didn't particularly rate in a sales environment go on to be very effective and successful trainers. I invariably tend to reach a quick conclusion on a trainer's credibility and I know this is probably wrong.

One of the most senior people at Procter & Gamble UK when I started eventually became one of the European vice presidents before writing a book and facilitating a training package called *Thinking Outside the Box*. Whilst he clearly achieved great success in his Procter & Gamble career and afterwards, I was not too impressed when I attended one of his training sessions at Kellogg's. I introduced myself and asked why he hadn't used the ideas he was presenting back at Procter & Gamble, citing some examples where we could have responded to competitive threats more effectively. I don't think he was too comfortable with my questioning and didn't provide much of an answer.

There have been occasions where I have needed much more patience to fully appreciate the benefits someone can provide and there have also been occasions where I'm convinced that someone is 'stealing a living'.

The great thing about Procter & Gamble training was that it was invariably delivered inhouse by colleagues and managers that you saw regularly. This meant there was continuity of materials and most examples and role-plays were appropriate to your day-to-day job. Often when external training companies are introduced, they shoe-horn the client into their existing programmes. Some do this very well as they invest time in understanding your people and business model, whilst others just put your corporate logo on the page and use the same materials for everyone.

Training programmes can also reflect the character and views of the person who commissions the training, and they can sometimes hold quite subjective views on the people to be trained and what they require. This can at times lead to the wrong type of training organisation being used. Experienced managers often refer to their own network for training providers and I have personally seen this be highly successful, but occasionally not work with programmes being cut short. I have also seen people with little experience or understanding of training and a questionable attitude towards others, become manipulated by training providers. They are persuaded to invest a lot of their budget on plans that require too much, too soon from the trainees, who then become disengaged. A vicious circle can develop as people labelled as 'weak performers' are also seen as having the wrong attitude and a resistance to learning when the original decisionmaker cannot accept their own misjudgement.

At Procter & Gamble, training and personal development was a priority from day one. In contrast, when I joined Kellogg's, the sales team had been starved of appropriate training for several years and the new sales director realised that an effective training programme was essential for them to compete. He secured the investment and introduced various programmes aimed at improving functional competency and leadership amongst the more senior group. I particularly enjoyed and benefitted from the latter with insight into concepts like 'Alpha Leadership' (in this case, the art of leading consciously, captured by Robert Dilts—not to be confused with alpha male leadership styles—which may be appropriate in some environments, but in business I deplore) and the Beliefs of Excellence. The follow-up one-to-one coaching was enlightening and powerful.

AG Barr was different. The commercial director had started to introduce some competency-based sales training, which I supported when I arrived twelve months later. The prevailing culture though was that training was viewed almost as a punishment. You were sent on a training course if you were not very good at something. It took a long time to try and reverse this view and get people to understand the principles of positive, proactive personal development as opposed to corrective, punitive activities. Occasionally, the latter perspective prevailed, ironically with some who had progressed rapidly but developed a slight sense of superiority.

One thing I have always realised about training is that there is usually way too much to remember on a course. The power is usually through the key points that stick with individuals and the thoughts they provoke. A training provider used by AG Barr, Making Business Matter, differentiated their offer by a concept of reinforcing learning through 'Sticky Pieces' follow up. An innovative approach so long as the training beforehand is sufficiently spread out and doesn't take over the day job. People usually learn best at their own pace and through subsequent experience. Training rarely delivers a full improvement 'lock, stock and barrel'.

Lattes and Learning

Certain types of training are much better done together, face to face. However, so much training is also now online so why should people need to do it at their desk or in a training room? More and more managers let their teams learn at home. As an alternative, I introduced learning-oriented coffee mornings (hotel lobbies can be great for this).

Following the disruptions caused by the Covid-19 lockdown, applications such as Zoom and Microsoft Teams have been appreciated by a much broader audience and have undoubtedly led to a change in attitudes and behaviour towards people working from home. There have been many articles posted on LinkedIn to this effect, including one I posted myself which reached over ten thousand views. A hot topic in the autumn of 2020.

A few points to ponder

- **Some of the most effective training is delivered inhouse since the trainers know the business and your role within it.**

- **Objectivity and experience are important when commissioning training.**

- **Training should be positive and proactive, not punitive.**

- **Focus on a few key learnings to take from training programmes, you will never remember it all.**

- **The best external training takes participants to a new dimension.**

Coaching

Some training is specifically to teach a process or develop a skill, but most of the learning occurs outside the 'classroom' and is most effective with a strong coach.

The International Coaching Federation (ICF) defines coaching as partnering with clients in a thought-provoking and creative process that inspires them to maximise their personal and professional potential. My purpose is not to provide extensive guidance on coaching—there are plenty of specialists who can do this to great effect. A few simple observations of coaching are captured below and within scenarios, as we progress.

Coaching is often about providing the right support, in the right environment, at the right time. For some, it is almost as natural as breathing, but for others, it requires more conscious effort. Procter & Gamble were extremely focused on managers being coaches and typically tended to excel in that field. One of the principles was that managers should be assessed on the quality of the people they train, or words to that effect. Remarkably similar in sentiment to Simon Sinek: 'the greatest contribution of a leader is to make other leaders'. However, other organisations I've worked with have lacked the personnel and experience to coach successfully.

At various times I have observed managers confuse micromanagement with coaching and have become somewhat dismayed at how people have been treated and their confidence eroded. Coaching is providing freedom but keeping a supportive arm close by. It is like removing stabilisers from a child's bike and keeping hold of them as they start to pedal until they can do it themselves. It is about sharing a framework or structure and then encouraging people to use it, develop it and make it their own through timely and constructive feedback.

Coaching is not about poring over every piece of work produced, correcting, or changing trivial details and manipulating it into your own style. I despair at the times I have seen unfocused senior managers in important meetings, constantly referring to their laptops to proofread their teams' work as they lacked trust and faith in them. Or worse, because they were so arrogant that they did not view others' efforts as ever good enough.

Mentoring

For me, mentoring should be a very personal and natural process. I am never comfortable with the idea of mentors being appointed or allocated; that is too contrived and more like indirect management. A mentoring relationship usually builds on an existing personal relationship. If it needs suggesting to someone that they should mentor a junior member of the team, then I believe the point is being missed. Relationships in business can grow between people of different levels, or different functions when a connection forms naturally. Mentoring can then naturally occur without the word ever being used. If someone goes around telling others that they are a mentor to someone, I usually interpret it as looking for credit and recognition for themselves. I've supported literally hundreds of people during my career and in the vast majority of cases, I have made sure that I'm there in a mentoring capacity if and when needed, on both a proactive and reactive basis without the M-word being mentioned. Similarly, there are always people I am comfortable turning to myself for help and advice, both within my own organisation and externally.

Exploitation

On a couple of occasions, I have witnessed a situation which I have been really uncomfortable with, where a senior manager in an organisation develops a friendship with a more junior and often newer employee. They may not always work on the same team, or even in the same department but the more experienced party sees skills and attributes that can enhance their work and improve their standing in the organisation. In most cases, this just develops into a genuinely supportive, mentoring relationship that benefits both.

Unfortunately, this can develop in a more sinister way where the enthusiastic, eager individual is desperately keen to impress and becomes a victim as the more senior figure finds them easy to exploit. The honest, ambitious individual is flattered by the attention and does more and more to secure recognition but eventually gets so taken advantage of that it borders on bullying. I have known people working until midnight and then being called to a manager's house over the weekend to improve and polish their presentation for a customer or a conference. The manager gets the plaudits and the individual gains very little. The same can happen over and over again and whilst it might be tempting to suggest the victim should 'grow a pair' or 'man up' and refuse, saying no in business is something that many people find really hard. In my view, the more senior figure is clearly the villain and with greater emotional intelligence they would understand this is not an appropriate way to treat colleagues.

Of 'Hodds' and Men

Readers would be surprised to learn that former England football manager Glenn Hoddle had a career in FMCG! Of course, *the* Glenn Hoddle has been a football man since he signed for Tottenham Hotspur aged eight. However, in terms of analogy, I have witnessed his alter ego on several occasions during my career.

Without a doubt, Glenn Hoddle was one of the finest, most skilful, and technically gifted English players of all time, but as a coach, he was not able to use those skills as effectively.

Over the years, several players he coached or managed have referred to his reported habit of needing to be the best on the training ground, which did little for morale. 'If he were chocolate,' said one England player, reportedly, 'he would eat himself.' The overarching impression is that here is a man who has never achieved the empathy that comes naturally to all great leaders. An effective coach he may be, but he's also a manager with a tendency to belittle players for their technical limitations through his eagerness to display his skills.

Gary Neville wrote, 'Hoddle took over from Venables and it's been said before: if only he had possessed the man-management skills to go with his undoubted football intelligence.' It has also been said that Hoddle tends to blind his players with science, overanalysing to a point where those listening tune out. Tony Cascarino described the effect of Hoddle's man-management as 'grown men feel as if they are being treated as children'. He would call team meetings, ask for players' input and then tell them that they were wrong.

I have had the pleasure and privilege of working with some incredibly talented and clever individuals. I have respect for them, but no one is ever perfect! Some have displayed 'Glenn Hoddle Syndrome' and I am sure I have done so myself on many occasions. In fact, I have done so deliberately in the introduction, in my description of people management!

Some people are comfortable making connections with others and leading them. Many clearly are not and the idea of managing people is incredibly daunting for them. Likewise, to someone like me, building a complex interlinked spreadsheet with macros, pivot tables and complex formulas causes feelings of trepidation, to put it mildly! What is not hard for some, may be terrifying for others.

There is a common phrase that 'you shouldn't take people for granted'. To expand on that, nor should you take people's innate skills and abilities for granted as this can leave them frustrated, with diminished confidence and insecurity.

What Glenn Hoddle types need to consider, but are often blind to, is the impact they have on others. Colleagues and subordinates (great modern word—not!) can be left feeling demotivated and as if they aren't really valued. Like Glenn, there can be a tendency for managers to show 'one-upmanship'—where they seem compelled to outdo others in meetings with new insightful data or updates that are either unnecessary or add little value.

In addition, they will let people talk or make a point, and then move straight on to something else without acknowledging what they have just heard. This leaves people feeling confused or belittled since they have not been listened to.

Reference to Hoddle again—'he couldn't appreciate how those he was coaching just couldn't see what he was suggesting [vision] and do it naturally [technical skills]'. Some managers often 'throw' work at people accompanied by the phrase 'it will only take you fifteen minutes'. The manager may well be able to bash it out quickly, but it may take a day or more for someone else because it often comes on top of their existing workload. This just demonstrates a lack of appreciation for others' capacity and capabilities.

I have tended to be too trusting of people at times and have maybe shown a bit of 'Hoddlism' when assuming that people understand what I want or need them to do. If you ask someone to do something they *can't* do, that is a capability issue, and you need to provide them with the knowledge and support to gain the skills required. If it is something they *won't* do, you have an attitude and motivation issue to address. Sometimes we all need to take a step back and put ourselves in other people's shoes.

A few points to ponder

- **Micromanaging is not coaching.**

- **The most effective mentoring develops naturally from personal relationships.**

- **Providing opportunities for others is crucial but taking advantage of others' enthusiasm is deplorable.**

- **Everyone is unique. Recognise that we all have different strengths and weaknesses.**

- **Leaders and coaches should set the right example and keep raising the bar.**

- **However, continually outdoing others will not help a leader to improve the team.**

- **Determine if performance issues are 'can't do' or 'won't do' and respond accordingly.**

Feedback

Feedback and constructive criticism were early introductions in my Procter & Gamble career. The concepts had been well established there and whilst less formal feedback was an ongoing component of coaching, formal broad-based feedback as it was known at Procter & Gamble, was a familiar process at performance review time. Seeking feedback on how you operated from peers, managers, and others you interacted with soon became the norm. The feedback was open and transparent so you could see how others viewed you. However, capturing the feedback in a clear yet constructive and diplomatic way challenged some more than others. One person was particularly direct with feedback and caused a bit of an incident by writing in a colleague's feedback, 'Mick has a tendency to just piss people off'. The recipient was aggrieved and the writer somewhat indignant. The aim should be to be honest and direct, but also polite. Such nuances escaped many!

A phrase has been developed that 'feedback is a gift' and should be appreciated, but to me, the value only comes if it is considered and well-communicated feedback. I agree that feedback can be a gift, but you can choose to unwrap it and then still decide whether you will actually play with it. I have seen examples of terribly conceived feedback where the intent was positive, but the impact quite destructive. I have also observed feedback being used to 'stick the knife in' or belittle others.

Whilst comfortable and familiar with the concept at Procter & Gamble, at Kellogg's and latterly AG Barr, the introduction of feedback was quite a revelation. Various feedback methods, sometimes deployed at different hierarchical levels, are used by training companies and personal coaches the world over. For example, *360-degree feedback* is common terminology and can be a very, very in-depth process typically facilitated online by third parties from outside your organisation. More simplistic versions include *What Went Well/Even Better, If (WWW/EBI) feedback* and *Stop, Start, Continue*.

At Kellogg's, the first formalised feedback was anonymous. You chose a selection of immediate peers, your boss, your direct reports, and others you worked with to provide the feedback. Of course, you could work out which were your boss's comments and occasionally identify others by their writing style. One particularly challenging and often quite obstreperous individual was too lazy to shift between upper and lower cases, so you always knew what they had said as it was all in capitals!

AG Barr was very different. The commercial director and I, who was also ex Procter & Gamble, had developed an informal feedback culture across the sales team. His comment that 'feedback is a gift' was well established, although sometimes in a jocular manner! However, it was only after about ten years that the wider organisation considered itself ready to introduce a more formal feedback process. Some interesting discussions took place to determine whether all the people were capable of receiving and acting on feedback appropriately. I often rolled my eyes at some overly paternalistic views.

When required to ask for feedback, I always wanted to ensure I would get a good balance from the people I naturally gravitated towards and those I didn't connect with quite as well or see 'eye to eye' with. I am not aware of anyone exclusively choosing from the latter group, but many deliberately set out to get the feedback from their 'mates' or those they saw in the same self-image. To me, this smacked of insecurity and not really embracing the principles. If two people at the same level in an organisation do essentially the same role, why would they not ask each other for feedback?

When I received the feedback, I usually divided the opportunities to improve (negative comments) into three broad areas. Firstly, something I considered essentially true and my self-awareness confirmed that I needed to work on. Secondly, something I hadn't recognised myself but was insightful and I should consider. Finally, there is the feedback that you honestly just don't agree with and I always believe that if you have strong self-awareness and personal consciousness you have the right to dismiss it.

When asked to give feedback on an individual I always made sure to give it due thought and consideration so that it would be of value and encourage the recipient, even if I didn't feel qualified to say a lot. On some occasions, it is also fair to decline an invitation if you really do not feel you can add value or insight. My general approach is to use real life examples to support the feedback, but you must get the balance right.

Too much praise and positive examples can risk inflating someone's ego. Too much criticism can destroy a person's confidence. I once needed to give stern guidance on one of my team's feedback to their direct report. For every positive point they gave (and there weren't that many) there was a brief supporting example. For the many negative points/areas to improve there were about three in-depth examples. The feedback made an average to good performer with a positive attitude look like a completely useless operator and caused them significant personal distress.

When I had to include Next Higher Manager comments on someone's review or manager feedback as part of a 360-degree process, I always took time to read through beforehand and refer to points people had acknowledged themselves. This shows that you have paid attention and are not just projecting your thoughts and insights onto them. I have witnessed managers routinely just add standard comments to everyone's reviews, or a set of comments not referring to any of the individual's or manager's commentary—a lazy approach that robs recipients of the opportunity to learn.

Some remain quite sceptical about the value of 360-degree feedback. To me, it is a very powerful tool but relies heavily on honesty, self-awareness and good communication skills. Without those factors, it can be damaging.

Finally, there is always the potential for people to manipulate the use of feedback to try and enhance their own position rather than help to develop others. I was particularly irked by one manager who used to encourage their team to share their weekly 'wins' and achievements on a Friday afternoon. Several people would conclude their week with an email summarising the progress they had made and the challenges on the horizon. This was good practice in sharing learning, celebrating success and developing an *esprit de corps*. I was on the copy list and would occasionally recognise performance and results that caught my eye.

Unfortunately, the leader of this team had an incredibly annoying habit of reading through them all on a Saturday morning, giving feedback to each sender. This all sounds quite admirable; however, I was not convinced that it was because they had too much to do and no time during the week. To me it was more a slightly disingenuous demonstration of commitment to the cause, to show how dedicated they were. The actual feedback provided was basically 'good job, well done' to each report, mostly not personalised to the individual and invariably not specifically responding to anything that was reported. It was just lazy and added no real value at all. Whilst some of the junior members of the team may have been thrilled by warm words from the manager, most just saw it for what it was—cheap.

A few points to ponder

- **Feedback is a gift, but you can choose whether or not to unwrap it!**

- **Providing feedback is to help a person to improve, never to 'score points'.**

- **Feedback should be provided properly or declined politely! There should be NO in between!**

- **When providing feedback to others, remember the wise words of Yoda, the diminutive Jedi Knight: 'Do or do not. There is no *try*.'**

The MacGregor Dilemma

Management and motivational theory continue to be developed and I make no claims of academic excellence in the field. Yet I have always found there to be real merit in some of the simpler, more historical theories espoused by the likes of MacGregor and Maslow, which in my experience continue to be relevant today.

Writing in the early 1960s, Douglas MacGregor developed his contrasting Theory X and Theory Y model that explained how managers' beliefs about what motivates their people can affect their management style. Theory X is the authoritarian approach and Theory Y is more participative.

Those who believe that team members inherently dislike work and have little motivation, according to McGregor, are likely to use an authoritarian management style. This approach tends to be very hands-on and usually involves micromanaging people's work to ensure that it gets done 'properly'. McGregor called this Theory X.

On the other hand, those who believe that people take pride in their work and see it as a challenge are more likely to adopt a participative management style. Managers who use this approach trust their people to take ownership of their work and do it effectively by themselves. This is Theory Y.

Experience suggests to me that X and Y are endpoints on a spectrum. Again, if X is white and Y is black, there is a lot of grey in between. Different types of work (physical, manual, analytical, cerebral), different work environments (public sector, private sector, large established corporations, SMEs, entrepreneurial businesses etc.), and different motivators and reward structures can all influence behaviours towards X or Y. Similarly, different challenges or situations can require flexibility of style and approach. For example, more Theory X behaviours may need demonstrating when a crisis mentality is required, and people need to carry out specific instructions or complete tasks efficiently and effectively. A typically more Y-orientated manager may need to adopt a more hands-on approach at this point, but where interpersonal relationships are strong, this temporary style would be understood and accepted.

The American military introduced the acronym 'VUCA', standing for volatile, uncertain, complex and ambiguous, to describe the context of terrorist attacks and the Gulf War in the noughties. VUCA has since been applied to the rapidly changing business world with David Snowden and Mary E. Boone suggesting in the *HBR* that 'wise executives tailor their approach to fit the complexity of the circumstances they face'. Their work on the Cynefin framework explores this concept in much greater detail than I could summarise here.

Another area of growing debate surrounds consistency. Jack Welch once claimed that great leaders are 'relentless and boring' by remaining on-message, sticking to their commitment and demonstrating consistency in their decision-making. Another article I read in the *HBR* shares the principle of 'both/and' leadership and how in the modern (VUCA) world leaders shouldn't worry so much about being consistent as at the top, executives and leaders must be able to appreciate multiple, often conflicting truths. Again, I refer to the grey zone where I fully agree with the sentiment when the tailoring or inconsistency is sincere and constructive.

What frustrated me from time to time was seeing peers and colleagues engage in double-speak. In a managerial forum, some would clearly position themselves as advocates of Theory Y, for example, pushing a training agenda, talking about career development for individuals and improving organisational effectiveness. They would then go back to working with their teams and revert to Theory X! I have worked with people who almost seemed to have a split personality. They would 'wax lyrical' publicly about the importance of training, coaching and mentoring and then display very little understanding of what it meant day to day by micromanaging people, making snap judgements on individuals' potential (or lack of) and at times remaining aloof and dismissive of their direct reports and other colleagues.

Whether this type of behaviour is born of arrogance, insecurity, an absence of self-consciousness, or at times is a deliberate tactic of inconsistency to unsettle or keep people on their toes can be debated and of course will vary by individual. However, the impact on those they lead could be damaging. One person acquired the semi-jovial nickname of 'Der Fuhrer' by some of their team and when questioned about this insisted that they were quite happy with it!

A few points to ponder

- **Traditionally, most people respond best to consistent styles and behaviours from their leaders.**

- **In a VUCA world, strong leadership can require flexibility and tailoring of approaches so that 'sincere inconsistency' can be constructive.**

- **'Insincere inconsistency' is disrespectful and just 'playing games' with people.**

- **Practice what you preach!**

Hexagonal Pegs

In many organisations, people fulfil a specific function in a specific role and often become labelled with that. For example, 'she's an operations person' or 'he is a sales guy', 'they're just a marketeer', and so on. I was recruited by Procter & Gamble to join their sales department and that was where my career and progress was mapped out. A person could move between functions but typically that would be later in a career once someone had consistently demonstrated their ability. There were several moves from sales across to marketing as people wanted to broaden their skill set for a move into general management. Whilst I was at Kellogg's, the sales finance partner moved across permanently and became an incredibly good national account manager, before quitting for a much bigger job back in finance. Some companies recruit onto a graduate program where they initially spend time working in a variety of functions and then in conjunction with their management and HR, they focus on the area deemed the best fit. Clearly, there are merits and drawbacks to each approach.

It is not just on a departmental basis that some get labelled though. Within the sales environment colleagues and peers have been identified as a 'numbers guy', or a 'people person', or someone who is only good with customers and not seen to have strong enough leadership qualities to progress. A recurring descriptor to pigeonhole someone is 'not strategic enough'. I have been given that one a few times.

Of course, we do all have different skillsets and natural abilities and moving people between roles is not necessarily the right thing to do. In a business like Procter & Gamble that works hard to recruit top talent, most people join with ambitions to make it to the very top. It is over time that labels are picked up and many people are happy with them. The person who loves the cut and thrust of selling to customers can sometimes have little interest or motivation to fulfil a more planning or analytical role. Similarly, some people in sales just love managing and training teams of salespeople and do not want to spend too much time in front of customers. Someone from my early days in sales at Procter & Gamble eventually progressed to a global marketing HR role elsewhere.

Historically, people were reluctant to nail their colours to a particular (job) mast through fear of being seen as unambitious or not supporting the broader organisational needs. Today, thankfully, there tends to be more support and encouragement for people to be open and honest about the parts of the job they enjoy and want to do. The most mature realise that this could limit their opportunity to progress but accept the compromise.

For example, Jo Bloggs is strong in certain areas. This makes her a square peg but there are plenty of square hole roles in the business so she can continue to grow. Jack Bloggs is very much a round peg. There aren't many round hole roles in the business, so he will have to spend some time in a square hole if he wants to progress further.

I was always uncomfortable with people being labelled in this way by others, particularly when managers who had never worked with the individuals could have quite an input into their careers. I have heard managers with vacancies to fill say, 'I'm never having X in my team' because they are only good at this, or not good at that. My view was always that the manager should take responsibility to develop the areas where someone is weaker, not be dismissive and write them off.

Despite my protestations, I have been frustrated on occasions by someone else's preconceived ideas and intransigent views about a person being used to block that person from moving into a role. This tends to be found in those who have limited experience of developing people over time and accelerated progression later in their careers. I have taken belated satisfaction from this scenario on several occasions when those I have trained and supported have proved their doubters wrong.

Using the traditional example of square/round pegs and holes you could get too carried away and assign all manner of shapes to individuals and roles within a business, but that could get a bit silly. I would however draw attention to what I call a hexagonal peg. This is someone who has incredible ability and can be squeezed into a round hole or a square hole but never quite fits. I have witnessed a few great talents who were not truly considered as salespeople or viewed as real marketeers and moved through various commercial roles never fully delivering against their own or the organisation's expectations. For this reason, they often do not progress as fast as their peers with less ability and some managers don't have the patience or understanding to find them the right role. My view is simple—hexagonal pegs are few and far between. If you ever find you have one on your team, invest the time and energy to identify a hexagonal hole for them and it will invariably pay dividends!

A few points to ponder

- **You may have to make some compromises at points on your career journey but also need to be clear on your strengths and what you enjoy.**

- **The best managers embrace responsibility for improving all members of their team.**

- **If you inherit or unearth a hexagonal peg— cherish and invest in them!**

Seeing the Results

Ultimately, seeing people you have recruited, trained and developed progress in your organisation and go on to even bigger and better achievements is one of the best feelings in a business career. I've been in training and managerial positions pretty much since year one with Procter & Gamble. Whilst there have been the odd individuals whom I struggled to connect with, or very rarely didn't like at all, seeing people grow and develop has given me immense personal satisfaction and a real sense of accomplishment that financial reward and promotions genuinely don't match up to.

AG Barr was the biggest source of satisfaction as I was there the longest and in a senior position. Given that it wasn't a 'grad culture', there were many examples of people joining at sixteen or with few formal qualifications who had great potential but just needed backing and support to progress. Several of these 'ugly ducklings' grew into 'beautiful business swans'. They embraced change and bought into the training and coaching we introduced. Their talent and natural abilities, combined with a high work ethic, deservedly elevated them to the most senior positions in the sales function.

Procter & Gamble introduced me to a formula that captures this— the knowledge, skills and abilities (KSA) model. Performance is driven by an individual's knowledge, skills and attitude. In AG Barr, the 'ugly ducklings' had great knowledge of the business and great attitudes. What we were able to do then was drive their skills and competencies through a focus on development. And off they went to secure some outstanding achievements!

Of course, that isn't to say that graduates are any less worthy of praise; a university degree usually allows people to commence a career higher up the ladder. Their expectations are typically more overt than the bright people who haven't previously been encouraged or supported and hence have more covert ambitions. These individuals need a catalyst, and I was delighted to provide it.

Recognition

Recognition is often discussed (certainly in HR terms) with reward and remuneration, though this discussion is just about the importance of recognising a job well done, or someone's real efforts and commitment. Over many years I have looked upwards in organisations and been quite disappointed, concluding that those at the most senior levels in a business often just take people for granted. Some suggest that people are paid to do a job and may receive bonuses determined by the performance of the company and/or themselves. So why should they need or be given extra?

A fair point in many respects, but I am not concerned here about financial reward, more the human side of recognition and that simple emotion—gratitude.

I recall an occasion where not long after joining Procter & Gamble one of the most venerable members of the sales department, very senior to me at the time, but nowhere near the top of the organisation, was retiring. Through his long career, he had supported and encouraged the development of many of those currently climbing upwards. At one of his final meetings, his team presented him with an Everton Football Club shirt with his name and retirement age printed on the back. This was the early nineties, before the internet and easy ordering of such items, so it must have taken quite a bit of effort to arrange it. I remember thinking to myself what a lovely gesture this was and wondering if anything like that would ever happen to me in the future.

At one Procter & Gamble meeting just before Christmas, the division manager opened the day in the morning, and after running through the agenda, he called me up to the front. I wasn't sure why, but he proceeded to recognise my contribution throughout the year, thanked me for my efforts and handed me a bottle of champagne. I was thrilled with this recognition and returned to my seat beaming. He then called up someone else to do a similar thing and through the course of the day everyone was given a bottle of champagne. It was a lovely touch but of course, nobody ended up feeling particularly special!

Being American multinationals, both Procter & Gamble and Kellogg's had (rather twee to those in the UK) formalised recognition programs. Procter & Gamble's had the grandiose title of Global Chairman's Club Award or something similar. One of my managers and long-time mentors was flown to the head office in Cincinnati to accept one of these awards and I'm sure it meant a huge amount to him, but most people were not 'turned on' by the Global Chairman's Award. It was based on submissions from each country without really transparent criteria, so most regarded it as a political device and retained a level of cynicism. Kellogg's had a similar type of scheme and though I was part of a team that won for a World Cup in-store promotion in 2002, there was no trip to the States and the prize of a golden statuette of the Kellogg's founder invariably provoked a degree of mirth and mockery.

Retailers and wholesalers also issue awards to suppliers and the first one I ever received meant a lot at the time. Procter & Gamble's UK sales vice president contacted me one day to congratulate me as he had been sent an award from Asda CEO Allan Leighton to recognise a project. It was called Toiletries Champions and my team and I had executed it across Asda's store portfolio. The VP was impressed with the project results and the ABCD (Above and Beyond the Call of Duty) Award that had been sent through. This was typically an Asda internal recognition so we were one of the first suppliers to ever receive one. Later, Asda started to, in a colleague's words, 'hand them out like confetti to every Tom, Dick and Harry' at supplier conferences. This was a bit of a sour comment, but certainly, they did become distributed by buyers and buying managers, and were no longer sent from the CEO to sales vice presidents.

Other customers also used awards at conferences and gala dinners, but again, many viewed them quite cynically as there was no transparency. Most considered them meaningless or just a reflection of who had invested the most promotion monies or 'sucked up' to the buying team. The two awards we had great success with at AG Barr were very different.

The Bestway Wholesale Supplier of the Year and the Top Supplier Award from the Scottish Wholesale Association (SWA) both had open, clear scoring and adjudication. Plus, they included votes from staff working in the branches as well as cash & carries. They had clear, objective criteria and did not rely on arbitrary decisions behind closed doors. I take huge pride and satisfaction from leading teams who won both these awards on numerous occasions.

Awards like Bestway and SWA were presented at black-tie dinners where the emphasis was literally on celebrating success, a phrase that became more and more common in the later stages of my sales career, though I'd say it was more of a buzz phrase, often used without true conviction.

The most exhilarating example of celebrating success I witnessed was one afternoon in the mid-nineties when I was in Asda House in Leeds. Asda was still a PLC at the time, prior to being acquired by Walmart. CEO Allan Leighton had been presenting Asda's latest results to analysts in the city that morning and was heading into the office to brief everyone. Asda had great momentum at the time and was on a run of being able to report the 'fastest like-for-like sales growth in the industry'. Asda House has a large open atrium with balconies overlooking it on all four sides and as Leighton arrived, the balconies were filled with a noisy, exuberant crowd. It was a bit like being in an indoor arena for a music concert. As he stood with a microphone on the ground floor looking up and congratulating the Asda colleagues on another great set of performance figures, the atmosphere was electric. You could feel the energy and excitement buzzing all around!

Contrast that with the more conservative, restrained environment at AG Barr. On one occasion, at the first management board meeting of the year after we had delivered our best performance to date and were becoming highly regarded by analysts and investors in the city, a tray of bacon rolls was brought up to the boardroom to recognise the successful prior year. To be fair, the CEO had also arranged for a fried egg roll recognising that one of the team did not eat meat. Not quite as stirring as that day in Asda House!

Opus Dei

Metaphorically, on certain occasions, I have felt that some enjoyed crises more than success. Almost as if they yearned to be the FMCG branch of 'Opus Dei' with a predilection for corporal mortification. I have been a part of organisations that delivered fantastic results over many years though some people seemed more excited and stimulated by a crisis when they could set up War Rooms or Cobra Committees to pore over problems and their dire implications. Some misunderstand the concept of adopting a 'crisis-like' mentality (without a crisis). An *HBR* article on leadership reflected this by saying that most senior management teams 'thrive in a climate of adversity and derive great pleasure from pulling together and delivering'. This has certainly been the case in my experience, as celebrating the successful execution of plans has seemed almost frowned upon versus the deep-rooted gratification taken from trying to fix various setbacks.

On one occasion I worked with an HR colleague on a project to help managers understand simple ways they could acknowledge and recognise good work. I was surprised at how the culture had developed in some of the other functions and was a little incredulous at how some managers barely saw the need to even say 'thank-you' and extend common courtesies. One of the techniques I had regularly deployed of sending a ten-pound gift card and a thank-you note to someone's home address was seen by some as outlandish and unnecessary. I disagreed—a few in a year would hardly lead to a profit warning and recipients were typically very appreciative.

At a corporate level, the Barr culture could be a little introverted. However, salespeople enjoyed a bit more noisy and extroverted recognition, so I introduced some light-hearted sales awards at our annual national sales meeting. Some awards were more serious and nominated by people's managers, but the real fun was when we got into the 'most bizarre choices of company car' and 'best-dressed awards'. These were a tad tongue in cheek and the result of opaque deliberations, but I did see people referencing titles like 'best business result' and 'best newcomer' in their performance reviews and even on their CV. However, it was probably the bottle of prosecco that was most appreciated.

When Success is Not Celebrated

*'The greatest gift of leadership is a boss
who wants you to be successful'—Jon Taffer*

One of the Procter & Gamble principles that stuck with me was that managers should be assessed on the quality of the people they recruit, train and develop. I have always taken an immense amount of pride and pleasure in seeing people who I once trained, or who worked in my team, go on to wonderful achievements. Many of those I've coached have gone on to have fantastic careers, leaving my progression in their slipstream as they have risen to the highest levels of global organisations, founded and developed their own businesses and been successful MDs and entrepreneurs. I consider it a privilege to have played some part, however small or brief, in helping them get there. I never, ever resent their success.

Unfortunately, there are some people that I call 'Uncle Joes'—referring to Franklin Roosevelt's nickname for Josef Stalin. Uncle Joes occupy positions of influence and control over others, are sometimes quite dour and invariably resentful and suspicious. They value and appreciate the results that their top people deliver, but they inwardly dislike the respect and popularity that charismatic and successful people build with those around them.

Sometimes it gets to the point where they resent a person so much that they seek to marginalise or remove them, even if that comes at the detriment of performance and organisational culture. This isn't just at lower or middle management levels; it can go right to the very top.

At the end of the Second World War, Field Marshall Zhukov was recognised, lauded and celebrated as the man whose military exploits had freed Mother Russia from the Nazis. Stalin had publicly thanked him forty-one times during the conflict. He was the people's saviour, a hero of the Soviet Union. He had a bright future.

So, what did Uncle Joe do?

Celebrate him? Reward him? Fete him?

No!

Stalin banished him into obscurity.

Zhukov got lucky. Stalin could have just as easily had him removed 'for good'. Once Stalin had died, Zhukov was able to return.

Some people in leadership positions constantly feel threatened. They don't have the ability or awareness to truly appreciate, harness and utilise those whose skill set is different from their own. Particularly when it comes to managing and motivating others. To them, power is power. The concept of 'vulnerability is power' is as alien as the landscape on Jupiter. Despite someone's strong track record and what they contribute to the bottom line, rather than developing them and driving a positive culture, they choose to just get rid of them.

Who would want to work for Uncle Joe?

A few points to ponder

- **People appreciate being appreciated. They don't appreciate feeling taken for granted.**

- **Money is clearly important. However, there are other effective forms of recognition.**

- **Sometimes just the words 'thank you' are enough.**

- **Awards can offer huge motivation but can also have the opposite effect.**

- **The most credible awards have clear, objective criteria.**

- **Watch out for Uncle Joe.**

CHAPTER 4

BAKED ALASKA

Reflecting on university and my business studies degree, I recall being a little perplexed in the Management of Operations module on the curriculum, when we discussed the different roles or experiences that being part of an organisation can provide for people. The one that stood out was the 'sense of belonging and personal security' principle, where an organisation can act as a comfort blanket. Over time I came to realise what this meant and on my final day with AG Barr someone captured the concept perfectly.

Just after I joined, we moved the offices out of a relatively decrepit factory into brand new modern office space on Middlebrook Business , just near Bolton Wanderers' (Reebok) stadium. The board appointed me as the site leader to manage the transition and act as the figurehead for all departments on the site going forward. It wasn't perfect (at one point you could never get a parking space!) but over time we developed a great environment where people were generally very happy to come to work. Simple, small things made a difference. I always toured the office at some point each day just to say hello, check how people were and ensure that everyone, not just my direct reports, was comfortable to approach me if needed. Obvious things like a Christmas lunch, a night out and office doughnuts from time to time were of course well received. We reached Investors in People (IIP) silver status and invariably recorded the highest site scores in the company's annual employee engagement survey.

On that last day, one person who'd had more than their fair share of personal setbacks told me that getting through those challenges had a lot to do with coming into the Middlebrook office, which they described as a 'sanctuary'. They thanked me sincerely for providing the leadership that had created it. I had feelings of intense pride and a true sense of fulfilment when I heard this. It was possibly my most poignant lesson in motivation since I had first tried Baked Alaska.

The Dessert Menu

I had joined Procter & Gamble straight from university after a summer as a holiday rep for Saga (working with elderly people really did teach me a lot about patience and maturity!). After a year as an account executive working in the field, I was promoted and joined the grocery discount team (or 'disco gropers' as we were affectionately known). I worked for a seasoned sales manager who had singlehandedly developed Kwik Save into a major customer. He was now about to hand over some responsibility to a new inexperienced account manager and I knew he was a little nervous. Kwik Save had a very aggressive reputation and he didn't want me messing up the business.

I was desperate to impress him and paid avid attention during the training for the role. We spent a lot of time together and got to know each other quite well. I remember telling him once in conversation that I had always been fascinated by the dessert Baked Alaska as to make it, you put ice-cream into a hot oven. However, I had never actually tried it.

A few months later we had an out-of-office 'away day' where we stayed overnight in a nice hotel in Northumbria. The hotel had printed a bespoke menu for our meeting and the dessert was Baked Alaska. I looked at my boss who returned me a warm smile. He had listened, remembered, and made a relatively simple gesture, but I'd have 'run through a brick wall' at that point if he'd asked me to. Metaphorically, I slept wrapped in a warm comfort blanket that night.

The Power of the Pizza

Not long after Baked Alaska, I started to appreciate the importance of another culinary gesture in building a sense of belonging—I call it 'The Power of the Pizza'. Like many offices and workplaces, when we had a lot of people on site for meetings, a buffet lunch would be provided. Some would tuck in without reserve whereas others (myself included) would pick and fuss at whether the sandwiches had cucumber or mayonnaise on them or grumble that the crisps were only ready-salted. Some people would ignore the buffet completely or bring their lunch as usual. In the end, there was always waste. I am sure that most readers will have experienced something similar.

One day I asked the PA responsible for the site if we could have pizza delivered instead of a buffet. As the delivery arrived, the smell of pizza wafted through the office. Virtually everyone wandered from their desks to the meeting area, filled their face with pizza and chatted together for fifteen minutes or so. There was a spark in the office that day and not even a slice of green pepper was leftover. Ever since, over nearly thirty years, I've often deployed the power of the pizza at team meetings and office briefings—it brings people together like nothing else (there's always someone who doesn't like pizza though, so order a few portions of wedges and nuggets too!).

NB: Krispy Kreme Doughnuts also work well and were set up in the UK by another Procter & Gamble alumni!

The Wild Geese

As I developed throughout my Procter & Gamble career, I eventually headed up my first full sales team from a site right on the edge of the Procter & Gamble world at Skelmersdale, Lancashire. They had a health and beauty products distribution centre, also home to the small northern national accounts team which I was appointed to lead. The team consisted of a couple of experienced, wily campaigners mixed with a sprinkling of eager and enthusiastic graduates (including Greg Jackson, who is now CEO of Octopus Energy) and a wonderful PA. The three and a half years I had there were magical—I learned so much and had great fun.

As a small team based 'up north' out of sight of the head office in Weybridge, Surrey, we were effectively autonomous, 'off the grid', and within reason could behave as we wished. We worked hard, delivered some excellent results and didn't take ourselves too seriously.

After seeing a fabulous video produced by Saatchi & Saatchi at a planning meeting, I persuaded them to get me a copy to share with the team as I truly believed that it reflected the way we were operating. The video was *Lessons from Geese* and anyone can now see versions of it on YouTube. The original Saatchi version still brings a lump to my throat as the team embraced it as an authentic representation of our working philosophy and *modus operandi*.

An idea came from within the team that we should use the geese analogy to create a team vision and mission statement. Everyone in the team gave input and we reworked and word-smithed it until everyone was happy before getting it professionally printed. It then took pride of place in our office and on our desks. The UK general manager came to visit the site and was enthusiastic about the culture and down to earth environment we had developed.

One of the ideas we took from Asda was the idea of a red baseball cap to wear at your desk as a 'do not disturb' sign when you were concentrating on something. One of the team took the initiative to get personalised caps for each of us. Mine was embroidered with Saint Steve—well, I am from St Helens after all!

When a new general manager was appointed, he shared with everyone his vision for how he wanted the business to run, the type of environment he wanted to create and the support and co-operation we needed to share. His comments closely mirrored what we had created so I sent him a copy. I was disappointed to never receive any feedback about this and moved on from Procter & Gamble soon after.

Tea, or Is It Dinner?

An instance that affected me negatively was at one of my first sales conferences. During the afternoon break, I remarked to a colleague that I was really hungry and wondered aloud what we would be having for tea. A more senior figure whom I hardly knew, turned around and said quite sneeringly, 'Tea? Tea? Good Lord, you're working for Procter & Gamble now. Your evening meal is called dinner.' While this may seem trivial to some, the effect of this put-down lingered and drove at the heart of my personal insecurity. I didn't feel a great sense of belonging at Procter & Gamble that day and on a later training course learned that this was probably an example of tertiary discrimination. Ever since, I have endeavoured to always give new starters, in particular, a warm and inclusive welcome, whichever organisation I worked for.

Acronyms

I have often heard that joining a new business can be like learning a new language as all organisations have their own phrases, terminology and acronyms. And that is before you get to know the marketplace dynamics and the characteristics of the brand or products. It can be difficult to fit in and remember what everything stands for, but, typically, you get there over time. Once you are familiar with the business language and colloquialisms, you start to feel a greater sense of belonging. FMCG is full of acronyms—a unique language with individual company dialects.

Weekly Awards

Acronyms do also occasionally provide an opportunity for mischievous or immature fun. We had a weekly 'huddle' at Kellogg's (the idea being borrowed from Asda) where everyone in the sales team who was in the office would come together to share important updates and celebrate success. Either the sales director or one of the sales leadership team (SLT) would lead the session and after a while, someone suggested that we should recognise individuals' contribution to the team more formally. Again, inspiration came from Asda that had introduced a golden cone parking system years before, where great results or strong performance would be recognised by reserved parking at the front of the building or use of the company Jaguar for the week. All agreed it was a good idea, but it needed a name or identity. Kellogg's liked to bring their brand characters to life across the business, so somewhat mischievously, with Frosties in mind, I suggested Tony's Weekly Award for Teamwork. After a while, someone realised what this would look like when converted to an acronym!

A colleague brought up in an SLT meeting that they were pleased that one of the secretarial team who never appeared particularly engaged with the business had really responded to the huddle and been spotted taking notes. Impressed and intrigued, one of the sales controllers elected to stand near her at the next one and peered over her shoulder as she wrote. I don't remember the exact details, but the notepad read something like: frozen cod, minced beef, new potatoes, 2x beans, fairy liquid, bread rolls, cheese, etc. She was writing out her shopping list!

Agent of Change

One of the reasons I had been recruited by Kellogg's was to support a cultural change. I had expected Kellogg's, as a market-leading US multinational, to be similar to Procter & Gamble in terms of culture, systems and business processes. They were both supporters of huge iconic brands with high levels of marketing investment and a commitment to research and development. However, I think it is fair to say that in many ways Kellogg's was way behind Procter & Gamble. It was quite staid, autocratic and did not seem particularly committed to learning, development and career pathing. The new sales director had been an internal appointment and was keen to modernise the department's thinking. In contrast to Procter & Gamble, Kellogg's were always prepared to also recruit externally.

For a period before my arrival, the UK Head Office in Old Trafford had apparently been 'overrun' by management consultants helping to devise a strategy and implement a plan to transform the old approach to a New Kellogg's that was more fit for the future. This had involved some re-structuring with job losses through early retirement and roles becoming redundant, whilst new roles were identified to be filled from within or externally (hence my arrival).

At this time, as the new millennium beckoned, the grocery marketplace was undergoing radical change as Tesco continued to strengthen, Asda had been acquired by Walmart, Sainsbury's was trying to define a new way forward and Safeway was struggling to remain relevant and independent. Therefore, Kellogg's were absolutely right to shake themselves down and equip themselves to compete effectively in the future. They had launched snack bars and breakfast alternatives such as Rice Krispies Squares and Nutri-Grain, and had acquired Lender's Bagels, but internally I found the environment quite tough to settle into. There were clear divisions within the existing team between people embracing the change and those being dragged along reluctantly. The phrases 'new Kellogg' and 'old Kellogg' were bandied around as badges of (dis) honour or used as verbal weapons in discussions. Ironically though, with the fresher eyes of someone new, it was typically the individuals I considered most old Kellogg who would swing the old Kellogg accusation back like a scimitar to win a point or belittle someone with more flexibility and a more open mind. It could be quite demoralising to observe and difficult to redress.

Focusing on the future, the sales director was very forward- thinking despite having developed in the old Kellogg environment. He really embraced the principle of personal development and investing in the team. Various training companies and coaches were engaged to support individual and team growth. To many, this all seemed eye-opening and innovative and I certainly benefitted greatly from some of the training and introduction to concepts like 'Alpha Leadership' and 'vulnerability is power'. However, I don't consider that Kellogg's were ready as an organisation to embrace some of the more radical or esoteric concepts at this time. I had some amazing experiences, worked on some great brands and met some extremely talented people at Kellogg's (although most moved on from the business quite quickly) but I never completely felt at home during my five years there.

The *What Counts* Factor

I have had thousands of pounds invested in my training and development by various companies which I appreciate. My career has taken me to some wonderful places, meeting incredible people and having some amazing experiences. However, it's the culmination of little or everyday things that counts, and these are the most effective way of building a true sense of belonging.

A few points to ponder

- **Things that cost little time or money and often get overlooked can have a significant impact on those you lead and those who work around you.**

- **Consideration, support and respecting others usually costs nothing.**

- **Never underestimate the Power of the Pizza (or the Doughnut)!**

- **Listen carefully. Remember what people say and if you can, identify a 'Baked Alaska'.**

CHAPTER 5

BEWARE OF THE BULL

For most people to progress in life and their careers, confidence is crucial. The ability to back themselves and have faith in their ability drives people to the top levels of achievement. However, some can struggle to differentiate between confidence and arrogance.

Francis Bacon proclaimed that knowledge is power, although of course this was long before the communication age and the internet. To some, throughout their career, having access to all the data and 'holding all the aces' is what provides the fuel for their self-confidence. Early in my career, I was introduced to the idea that performance is a function of knowledge plus skills plus the right attitude. Knowledge still comes at a price but access to it is now more readily available than for past generations. The video on YouTube called *Shift Happens (Did You Know?)* has been regularly updated from when I first saw it with even more incredible statistics about the amount of data generated around the world. In any meeting or discussion, the *modus operandi* of some is to know more than everyone else and continually drop in pertinent facts or updated information to show they are always in control.

One concern with this behaviour comes when they don't know the answer. Some may become hesitant, bluster, and feel vulnerable as they are unsure how to proceed. Some will recognise that they don't know and accept their exposure. Unfortunately, a minority will ride their reputation as 'all-seeing and all-knowing' to elaborate and even make things up as they go along. I have seen this happen regularly and depending on the circumstances and company they are with, many people are taken in. If the person is authoritative and uber-confident, few would be prepared to challenge them. For a while, even to their superiors, they can get away with it because they will 'romance' with such conviction. Eventually, though, people will get wise and the individual's credibility starts to be undermined. Being able to tell a story or paint a picture is an important part of leadership, but repeating, or telling a similar story to the same audience, quickly loses its impact.

Aside from decisions being made on flawed data, the other issue caused by this behaviour is the example it sets. Those working for them can start to mimic the behaviour and without having the necessary character, experience or emotional intelligence, can slip easily into arrogance, harming themselves and others.

In *Mind Games*, Neville Southall makes a telling observation that 'there are too many people doing jobs in which they have to pretend to be experts on subjects that they don't know enough about, and that leads to people leading others without the best tools to help them succeed'.

'It Isn't You'

Eighteen months or so after joining Kellogg's the MD moved on to a new role in the US. His replacement was an external appointment and while we were waiting for him to start, the sales director who had recruited me was also reassigned. In a meeting with the new MD to present our plans for the following year I made a comment that 'when we get a new sales director, whoever that may be…' The MD quickly quipped back, 'Well, I can tell you it isn't you.' I was qualified for the position and though I didn't expect it, the MD's comment was a bit embarrassing. A few people joked with me about it later.

I decided to book some time with him and ask for his feedback on *why* it wasn't going to be me and what I should do to be ready when the role came up again. His feedback was vague though he did suggest that a powerful tactic was to behave as if you are already in the position above. The person we expected to get appointed did indeed get the role and had repeatedly used that tactic, which created a lack of trust and other issues within our peer group. Clearly, there was evidence that this type of behaviour could work but it wasn't an approach I was at all comfortable with. I viewed it as somewhat contrived advice, a little bit disingenuous and a way to undermine trust. The MD was only in the role for about six months and his legacy was just a few other inappropriate comments and nothing of real substance.

Credibility

Equally as damaging as arrogance can be the impact on an individual's credibility when it all goes wrong. After identifying a real need for improved selling skills across AG Barr, a colleague and I developed and facilitated a bespoke sales training course, which we piloted with my direct reports, all senior and experienced sales managers. The pre-work for the training was a case study I developed requiring the trainees to produce a sales presentation that was to be sent in before the course. The idea was to share them with the group anonymously during the training, inviting feedback and critique. Whilst reviewing the submissions before the course I had a feeling of déjà vu that I'd already seen one of the documents. On close inspection, the content of two of the presentations was about eighty-five per cent the same, but pictures and graphs on one had been moved up and down and from left to right to make it look different. I had not seen such a blatant example of copying homework since high school.

When the presentations were pinned up for all to see in the critique session on the day, I could detect murmurings of incredulity that two were so alike. The team worked out for themselves what had happened, and one person's credibility was plainly shot. The person whose work had been copied was of course pretty angry and explained to me that one of their colleagues had asked for some guidance and they had shared their presentation to help them get started. After waiting for the culprit to come clean, I eventually confronted them in private a week or so later. I could not believe that they tried to brazen it out, indignantly denying the clear plagiarism. They left the company of their own volition not long afterwards.

Fairy tales are usually considered when dealing with children but I have often used examples with the teams I have led as there are great teachings within them. Think of *Rumpelstiltskin*. The story ends well enough when he melts into a tantrum as his name is revealed. However, why was the miller's daughter put through that terrifying and threatening ordeal? It was because her father had 'bull shitted' the king about her abilities and been called out! Similarly, in an iconic episode of the comedy series *Only Fools and Horses*, Del Boy secures a contract to renovate a huge chandelier in a stately home. In attempting to be accepted in higher social circles and pretending to be someone he wasn't, he makes claims that he patently doesn't have the skills or resources to deliver against. As ever, Rodney his younger brother calls him out, ridiculing Del by asserting that he can't restore the chandelier with 'Superglue and Windowlene'. Initially of course, just like the experienced manager on my sales course, Del brazens it out, although when Rodney is out of earshot, he asks Grandad if they have any 'Superglue and Windowlene'! If you have never watched this, it is a true comedy and carries a pertinent lesson for business.

Impostor Syndrome

Although grocery wholesale is often regarded as a male-dominated environment it has been refreshing to see the emergence of more and more female leaders. As most of AG Barr's business team managers in wholesale were female, I joined them in attending the 2018 Women in

Wholesale conference where I witnessed a powerful presentation from Hazel Detsiny, another Procter & Gamble alumna who has progressed to senior and influential positions at Unilever. Hazel talked about the concept and reality of impostor syndrome. For someone in her position as an MD to talk openly about this was inspiring and refreshing.

Impostor syndrome is a psychological pattern in which one doubts one's accomplishments and has a persistent internalised fear of being exposed as a fraud or impostor. It can be what drives bluster and bullish behaviours, or it can simply gnaw away at and undermine one's confidence. Early research focused on its prevalence among high-achieving women, although impostor syndrome has been recognised to affect both men and women equally. It takes courage and honesty to admit to these feelings, certainly in a 'data is power' type of culture.

Contemporary thinking has moved on from Francis Bacon, with the idea that vulnerability is power. If someone has a resolute and innate level of self-confidence, they are comfortable saying that they don't know or understand something and inviting those with more knowledge or understanding to enlighten them. They are prepared to show vulnerability in front of others. One CEO I worked with had a highly effective way of occasionally holding out his hands palm upwards and saying, 'I'm not the expert here', thus inviting the experts to contribute more and lead to a solution. It takes true strength and courage to allow yourself to be vulnerable.

Again, I like the straightforward way Neville Southall expresses his thoughts here: 'I know what I don't know. I don't have all the answers or even half of them. I know what I know and know how to use that to help myself and others, but I also know where my gaps are in knowledge and expertise. If you know what you don't know, it's far easier to be an open person than if you think you know everything.'

A few points to ponder

- **Performance = Knowledge + Skills + Attitude**

- **Confidence is a key component of a positive attitude, but as Neville Southall puts it, 'confidence is having the faith in yourself that you'll learn from your mistakes, not that you won't make any'.**

- **If you feel the onset of Impostor Syndrome, don't be too worried. It can affect any of us. It is how you deal with it that matters.**

- **Be mature, considered, honest and avoid the bull(shit).**

CHAPTER 6

POO, PEE & PERIODS

An immature title for a chapter about maturity

RBM

At one of my earliest sales launch meetings, the presenter stood up and began to share details of a crucial brand initiative. All the recent graduate sales intake sat together, and we were looking at each other bemusedly as the presenter kept referring to 'RBM'. Eventually, someone dared to put their hand up (it wasn't me) and ask what it stood for. The answer of 'runny bowel matter' was received to a chorus of giggles and disgust until the presenter told everyone to 'stop laughing—it makes us millions of profit!'. The brand was Pampers, and we were all issued with product demonstration kits to simulate soiled nappies with our buying contacts.

If that took a maturity stretch to deal with, the worst was yet to come.

What on Earth is a Catamenial?

There had been rumours that Procter & Gamble were going to launch into the catamenial or feminine hygiene category. For those who do not know, think tampons and sanitary towels. These are crucial products for a big proportion of the (female) population, but not items that most young males want to get involved with. However, you learn to grow up, be mature and take your responsibilities seriously. I ended up working with those categories for several years and my maturity was accelerated, certainly in my professional life.

It was a touch embarrassing to take a silver attaché case into a meeting with a female buyer and open it to reveal knickers, sanitary towels, and vials of blue water to allow you to demonstrate the product's absorbency. However, there is a serious job to do and you are focused, determined and ambitious. In contrast, there is humiliation when you forget to remove the said sampling kit from your car boot and 'the lads' discover it at the weekend!

One Friday afternoon as I sat at my desk, I was working on various projects including the launch of new Always pantyliners (whose USP reflected that they contained zeolite crystals). My mind was starting to wander towards the weekend, but I was suddenly snapped back to reality and could not quite believe what was written in a document I was studying. One of the reasons Procter & Gamble became one of the most successful businesses on the planet was their commitment to research and development and their deep understanding of consumers. Nothing in Procter & Gamble is done on a whim or by chance—everything is thoroughly researched and analysed. You did sometimes see detached clinical logic lacking a touch of common sense though!

In the document, there was a graph headed: 'Sniff Tests on Used Pantyliners'!

All manner of unpleasant thoughts came to mind as my maturity temporarily regressed, especially at the thought of who conducted these tests. Eventually, I found out that they were done in Italy, sometimes by experienced wine tasters who had a sense of smell attuned to the delicate aromas in the wine! For the record, the zeolite crystals' role was

Leadership, Levity and the Power of Baked Alaska

to absorb odours and before I used the graph in the sales presentation, I used a little common sense and changed the title to 'Odour Emittance Analysis'.

MBW

By the time I was introduced to MBW, I had matured sufficiently to just get on with the project without silliness or histrionics. MBW stands for mild bladder weakness and the product, Certina, was targeted at females with occasional incontinence. Prevention of MBW is one of the reasons pregnant women are encouraged to perform regular pelvic floor exercises. As ever, comprehensive research had identified a consumer need and with their expertise in nappies and sanitary towels, Procter & Gamble had the necessary manufacturing experience. My role was to set up a test market in Aberdeen by securing the participation of the key retailers and monitoring product sales as the marketeers tested various communication methods. The TV advert was shown in the Grampian region and was typical Procter & Gamble—highlight a need and provide a solution. It showed a woman encountering the discomfort and embarrassment of MBW when sneezing and laughing, but new Certina was the perfect discrete answer.

I was ultimately relieved to hand over responsibility for nappies, feminine hygiene and MBW to someone who one day would become my boss in another company.

A Day in the Shit

It would be difficult to tally how many days I've spent on training courses in various hotels and conference facilities. However, one day at an advertising agency in London will always stand out from my time in the marketing of cereals at Kellogg's. We had a project to look at introducing prebiotics to products to improve gut health and spent

71

literally all day being educated about poo and wind. There were some incredible facts on the day about litres of wind per day and weights of stool. The only other time I witnessed that much fascination with bodily waste was when I drove my six-year-old son and a few pals to a birthday party—for some reason, that was all they talked about in the back of the car.

Despite lapses like above, having been required to grow up and mature early in my career, years later I struggled to find one advertising campaign in AG Barr as amusing as most of my peers did. IRN-BRU ran a campaign centred on the premise 'IRN-BRU gets you through' with one of the television executions showing a dad whose wife and mother-in-law want to call their new baby daughter Fanny, needing IRN-BRU to help him come to terms with it. Whilst I appreciated the advertising idea, which was well received by the target audience, I wasn't particularly enamoured by grown men tittering about ordering point of sale materials and brand support items such as 'fanny magnets' and 'fanny packs'. I had either grown up at last or lost my sense of humour. The former I'd like to think.

The vast majority of people have careers where poo, pee and periods will never be discussed in the work environment, so what other lessons can be shared about maturity?

Personal Winning Strategy

As we go through our careers, we develop, often subconsciously, a personal winning strategy that has helped us to progress. It is a collection of behaviours, actions, values and attitudes that have delivered our personal successes and to an extent define who we are. Some people remain satisfied with this style and approach. There is nothing wrong with that, though there is a danger that as the world changes around you, your effectiveness may diminish. A style that has always delivered positive results may become less productive. What historically helped your career and development can start to hinder it. In some cases, this can lead to bitterness and resentment if the person isn't aware of the choice they've made as others move onwards and upwards if the person isn't self-aware of the choice they've effectively made. This was captured in 2007 by Marshall Goldsmith when he published *What Got You Here Won't Get You There*.

Some adapt and modify their style covertly whilst others may make more overt changes following training courses, feedback and coaching. When someone makes a conscious, overt choice to change it can prove difficult and artificial. It can reduce trust and credibility as the individual's sincerity is questioned. This creates a credibility gap. For example,

> *'Since going on that course, he now keeps coming to see me all the time.'*

> *'She must have been given some feedback because she's suddenly more friendly and polite.'*

> *'Their boss told them to change how they behave.'*

Others occasionally take this further and try to completely reinvent themselves. One person I worked with took great kudos from being known by their nickname early in their career. However, as they started to appreciate their own ability and their ambition to progress grew, they realised the nickname was an inhibitor and suddenly insisted on being referred to by their first name, correcting others in the process. They went from being fun-loving, gregarious and affable to suddenly behaving in far more considered, serious and introverted ways. It was not me, and I'd relate the story personally if it were, but for ease let's just say that it was me and 'Smudger' as I was called, trying to become Steven overnight. This caused a degree of suspicion and even ridicule with people making references to Prince, the pop star and musician who became The Artist Formerly Known as Prince. 'Steven' was talented and went on to have a successful career, though the metamorphosis was only complete once he'd left the company and the moniker 'Smudger' completely behind.

In his book *The Cold War*, John Lewis Gaddis describes how the Americans with so much respect for their coveted constitution initially found themselves concerningly disadvantaged against the Soviet Union. They viewed the Soviets as scorning their values of truth, honour, justice, consideration for others and liberty for all. The Cold War transformed American leaders into Machiavellians who resolved to 'learn to be able not to be good' themselves and use this skill according to necessity. The pressure to act tougher or be more assertive and aggressive can become a real burden on someone who fundamentally is not equipped to act in such a way. The CIA might have eventually relished the challenge in covert international operations deemed for the greater good, but in a business environment, people trying to be something they aren't rarely succeed in my experience.

One of the brightest, most considerate, and supportive people I worked with sometimes fell into this trap. They occasionally behaved as if to succeed and gain more respect they needed to consciously act more assertively and authoritatively, however, this only served to undermine their credibility. In a round of 360 feedback, they were upset when someone suggested they should 'stop acting like a captain of industry'. What they needed was some better coaching and feedback to make them more confident and effective with the unique skillset they had.

Consistency is Key

Youthful energy and experience boost confidence as you start a career journey and then maturity and experience provide more confidence later. It is the long time in between that many struggle with as they seek to understand who they are, what they enjoy and ultimately what level of progress is realistic (and some are never mature enough to see that).

In my early days at Procter & Gamble, we went on a lot of in-house training courses that were usually moderated by more experienced and senior managers. Given the high-potential, competitive graduates that joined Procter & Gamble, the beginning of these courses was a bit like the start of a Grand Prix where everyone scrabbled to be in front at the first corner. Their relative immaturity combined with naked ambition created a high-octane training cocktail. Each wanted to be recognised as the leader within their peer group by the senior figures who could support and accelerate their career. It makes sense, but personally, I hated it and would withdraw into my shell a little until there was a more appropriate opportunity to shine.

Some people lack the maturity to realise that the strongest leaders don't always need to lead overtly. They almost become addicted to being the leader. They can't help themselves, as they have an irresistible compulsion to lead and manage in every situation, within their own function and beyond. Whether it is general business planning, operational meetings or choice of pub or restaurant for dinner (or tea!!), they stride off in front like Peter Pan and expect everyone to sing, 'Follow the Leader, Leader, Leader'.

Two particular problems can arise from this. Firstly, they might not be as clever as they think and go in the wrong direction. Also, even when they are correct, it does not help others to learn and develop if they are always deprived of an opportunity to lead for themselves.

In a career, it is being competitive, consistent and considerate over the long term that earns respect and cements leadership, not fighting for attention at the start.

A few points to ponder

- We all grow, develop and mature during our careers.

- Our personal winning strategies should adapt and evolve covertly to ensure continued growth.

- Overtly reinventing yourself or adopting an alien style can create distrust and credibility gaps. This should be avoided.

- Be yourself, be mature and be comfortable in your own skin.

CHAPTER 7

THE ILLUMINATI

Don't worry, this section will not be investigating David Icke, Reptilian Super Beings or the Protocols of the Elders of Zion. It's not an assessment of corporate conspiracy theories (though Procter & Gamble attracted rumours of satanic links at one time, primarily due to their moon and stars corporate logo), but more an opportunity to highlight two words of fundamental importance to those seeking to develop high performing teams or build modern progressive cultures.

Decision-making

It is also important to note that there will always be a need for hierarchical decision-making in large organisations. Procter & Gamble had a training program called Decision Mapping. The basic concept being that business decisions require a combination of various evaluators to help determine the costs and benefits of different options and any number of implementors to make things happen, but ultimately there is only one owner of the decision. In large organisations, people at different levels are empowered to make decisions of varying magnitude and be accountable for the consequences. However, the biggest decisions will go right to the top with CEOs or chairpersons ultimately holding the casting vote in board meetings.

In a similar vein, there is often a need for confidentiality on sensitive matters within organisations. This can be for legal reasons, like 'insider trading' of stocks and shares when some officers have access to important results ahead of the market or proprietary knowledge and data of value to competitors. Again, board members have clear responsibilities which are why one morning in the autumn of 2012 when we arrived at our desks in AG Barr, we were greeted by a hastily written email explaining that AG Barr and Britvic plc were in advanced stages of a merger. Few outside AG Barr's and Britvic plc's boards knew about the discussions, so it was a big surprise to us all and had to be briefed to employees prematurely as a newspaper had obtained some details of it and gone to print. This would have been a major development in the UK grocery and soft drinks markets, though ultimately it did not come to pass. There is an interesting story as to why it did not happen, though this is best told by those who were closer to the proceedings.

So, acknowledging some of the limitations underpinning decision-making and confidentiality, two 'T' words are crucial in the way many organisations aspire to operate.

TRUST and TRANSPARENCY

(NB: There is a four-letter expletive with two 'T's often used when there is a lack of the above. I have heard the word used to describe several individuals during my career!)

I was particularly engaged in one leadership programme I attended, where we were introduced to Patrick Lencioni's *Five Dysfunctions of a Team* model. I would strongly recommend reading further material or watching videos of this on YouTube.

A degree of healthy tension among people in an organisation can spark creativity and help to solve problems. According to the *HBR*, 'the absence of conflict is not harmony, it's apathy', therefore, you need sufficient levels of trust to channel the conflict constructively.

The basic emphasis on trust and the importance of vulnerability struck a chord and I was greatly encouraged that, at long last, the way I had always tried (consciously and subconsciously) to treat people and go about my business was finally being lauded and recommended to my peers. I was in quite a paternalistic and 'knowledge is power' type of culture and observed a mix of delight, disinterest and disdain across my senior management and director peer group as the training developed.

A picturesque hotel on a glorious day was the perfect learning environment and we were tasked with using cut-up magazines and pictures to produce a collage representing Lencioni's ideas. And yes, we were getting paid whilst doing this! All manner of bizarre creations ensued, but the design most recognised and applauded was the large letter T that one attendee had produced. A simple and clear representation of trust. The irony was that the person who produced it was viewed by many as acting quite Theory X with their own team. They micromanaged their team and was considered to lack trust in any judgement except their own.

People can also make some comical attempts to keep your trust after they have tested it. A client recently cancelled some work at very short notice. In their brief email, they expressed that 'as a rule of thumb I don't normally let people down'—I immediately thought, 'Oh great, you've singled me out for poor treatment then!'

Psychological Safety

It is not always easy or wise to speak out, although it should be! I once shared a concern based on genuine observations in a meeting at my employers' head office. I expressed my worries that we had a growing morale issue, particularly across the other company locations.

The MD dismissed my suggestion as 'bollocks' and the room went silent. Tumbleweed time. No peers supported my comments, even though I knew from individual discussions that several held similar views. When scores from the next employee engagement report came in, most crucial measures had indeed declined.

It may be referred to now as 'psychological safety' but this is not a new phenomenon—think about *The Emperor's New Clothes* again. They all knew he was naked but it was only the naivety and inhibitions of a child that expressed the reality. People just didn't feel safe to speak up.

The Clique

It was at university where I first encountered the word 'clique'. I lived in a fully catered residence hall with over four hundred other students. Each year a president and other officers were elected to form a junior common room (JCR) committee to effectively run student affairs, for example, social events, the private bar and so on. However, new residents believed that aside from the JCR there was effectively a 'clique' of third-year students who in reality were in charge. These were a relatively small mixed group who, it was perceived, did not readily allow others to join them. I was elected president towards the end of my first year in 1988 and found that the clique wasn't really a clique at all—they were just a group of friends in their final year who kept themselves to themselves a bit more to concentrate on their studies. I engaged with them on several matters and they were helpful and supportive, but the idea of a sinister, powerful, closed elite did stick in my mind, coming to the fore again through Dan Brown's books years later!

As mentioned, how transparent any organisation can be is a matter of debate. Some things have to be kept confidential and shared on a need-to-know basis, whilst other things can be discussed and shared more openly. I always tried to be as open as possible with my teams and give everyone input whenever I could. I have witnessed cliques forming and managers having a disproportionately close relationship with one or a couple in their team, and it wasn't healthy.

One of the directors I worked with had one such close confidant that the rest of the leadership team regularly felt excluded. We would often be waiting for a meeting to start when the pair in question would arrive late or be seen having a quick one to one outside the room after which various outcomes would be presented to the rest of us as a *fait accompli.*

Similarly, groups can attend a meeting to discuss alternatives and make decisions. However, the boss, or a combination of the boss and their clique of closest confidantes, have already decided what is going to happen and the meeting becomes a sham. This lack of transparency and trust in the broader group leaves a lot of people feeling frustrated, isolated and insecure. Not a good culture at all.

I refer to small, tight-knit cliques who manage with a lack of trust and transparency as 'the Illuminati'. They form a small, closed group with a disingenuous level of influence on the proceedings of a department or function. Without transparency they ultimately only trust themselves, stifling the development and career progression of others.

Again, this can be born of arrogance (I/we know best), or insecurity (the fewer who know, the more we can control) or sometimes a complete lack of awareness. Whatever the reason, it does not build teamwork and Lencioni is right; trust needs to underpin everything.

'We need more honest discussion in business, less excessive politeness and politics.'

Melanie Healey, Retiring Group President, P&G / Verizon Board of Directors

Think long and hard about the following:

- **When trust and transparency are low, cliques and t**ts can flourish!**

CHAPTER 8

CONFLICT

The second of Lencioni's team dysfunctions refers to the conflicts that can arise in organisations.

Relativity

In analysing conflict, you need to first consider what defines it and this will vary by individual and within organisations.

Many agree that a level of healthy tension within a business is valuable. It stimulates challenge and growth. It prevents too much 'group think' and resists complacency setting in.

Problems arise when one person's healthy tension is interpreted or perceived as aggression or conflict by others. I am not aware of any recognised standards or calibrated scales to measure this—it is very subjective.

Some people, for multiple reasons, just do not have the self-awareness to understand the 'impact versus intent' dynamic of their communication or behaviours and thereby create conflict. In direct comparison, others may be particularly sensitive, less able to deal with routine challenge or disagreement and perceive conflict that isn't really there. Like many things, we have a spectrum to consider.

In managing this, most effective teams accommodate a combination of personalities, skills, viewpoints and styles that create and thrive on the healthy tension. However, when you have that combination, there is also greater risk of conflict unless there is real trust within the team— Patrick Lencioni territory. If there is trust and strong leadership, both bullish and bearish tendencies can be accommodated and utilised for the greater good. Similarly, personality differences highlighted through profiling (e.g. DiSC etc.) can be harnessed constructively and used to drive positive and productive output.

Internal v External Conflict

My career has mostly been working in sales and outward-facing roles dealing directly with customers. I always found external conflict easier to handle than differences and disagreements in my own company. Why ?

External conflict (i.e., with customers or other parties) tends to be quite overt. It is usually about financial matters or trading terms. Some people use conflict and exert pressure as negotiation tactics and whilst that can be challenging (and occasionally become personal) there is a clear and obvious reason for it—to get a strong result and satisfactory outcome. You may 'fall out' temporarily, but you typically move on once an acceptable agreement has been reached. The person you are dealing with externally has little direct influence on your career or reputation, especially if you secure an outcome that meets internal requirements. Whether there was conflict and how well you handled it is of little concern to anyone else (other than perhaps your boss or coach who should be there to help you improve).

Internal conflict of an unproductive nature or in an environment lacking trust can be much more covert and even sinister. It might just be that some people have different styles and 'rub each other up' the wrong way (e.g. in DiSC profiling the D (dominant) and S (steadiness) display opposite characteristics). However, there can also be much more to it than that. The metaphor 'stabbed in the back' implies a manifestation of more considered political conflict, sometimes initially hidden and subtle, but culminating in betrayal in meetings, the boardroom or a whispering campaign about you.

Ego and the desire to be (or be perceived as) top dog or leader can play a huge part, as can internal bias and prejudice. Sometimes, internal conflict can be driven by one personality. For example, people may have worked with the obstreperous individual who constantly seems to disagree, compulsively challenge everything and pick fights with anyone or everyone!

A Culture of Conflict

Developing a culture based on challenge (often leading to conflict) may be encouraged or even policy in some organisations. A colleague at Procter & Gamble once went for an interview at L'Oréal and was put off by, as they described it, the prevailing 'spirit of confrontation' that was heavily emphasised by the interviewer. Plans and ideas (and the person presenting them) were aggressively challenged to see if they would hold up, as opposed to the more supportive and nurturing environment that we had at P&G. Similarly, I know a few people who in the noughties worked in the Cauldwell Group, founded by British billionaire John Cauldwell. They were high calibre individuals, but their stays were brief as they couldn't settle into the high octane and at times quite 'brutal' environment.

Constructive criticism, even when it develops into a form of conflict can be a hugely powerful and positive tool but is a twin-edged sword that can be demotivational, destructive and damaging to an idea or an individual.

Taken to extremes, ongoing conflict can become bullying, which in days gone by was probably more tolerated in the workplace than in the more enlightened times we have now. Behaviours and comments quite common in the past would now be subject to a full-on HR enquiry. Nevertheless, damaging conflict still exists, though tolerance levels are thankfully lower.

As identified previously, conflict is a function of communication and some people will not take accountability for the consequences of what they say. If something isn't received positively and creates conflict, they make it all about the recipient and deflect responsibility. The following is a really powerful quote, again from Neville Southall:

> *'Part of the problem is the blurred line between "banter" and "abuse" and the mistakes people make when drawing that line. All I hear now is that you can't say a word to anyone "these days" for fear of causing offence or upsetting them, implying that nobody can take a joke. But that is simply not true. It just depends upon your relationship with them. The onus is on you to avoid offending, not on people to avoid being offended. The fault lies with you. Anything else is victim-blaming."*

From *Mind Games* by Neville Southall, former professional football (soccer) player and now social campaigner.

What are the Causes? Who Creates the Conflict?

One of the key things to identify when handling conflict is to find what is driving it.

Is it the obstreperous person who challenges for the sake of challenging, and if so, what causes them to do that?

It might be that it is someone with the knowledge and skills to perform well, but for some reason has an attitude that draws them towards a more challenging style resulting in continual conflict. It is probably the role of their manager or coach to try to understand and help them. It may be due to some insecurity or lack of self-confidence that makes them default to challenge everything.

Alternatively, it could be a deflection tactic as they lack sufficient knowledge and skills for their role but have an innate sense of superiority viewing 'attack as the best form of defence'. There are people who get to senior levels of organisations in this way, often leaving a divisive culture behind them. This is harder to coach and usually needs a senior and experienced third party to get the person to open up on why they adopt this approach before attempting to change.

Grievance or revenge can be a source of conflict. There are sometimes disgruntled individuals or groups of employees who seek to sabotage change and development. This particularly occurs when new people with different styles come into an organisation. I have personally experienced the difficulties caused by established individuals consciously rejecting and actively undermining the organisational, systems and cultural changes I was recruited to deliver.

It is important to try to understand the cause of this conflict and see if you can help and encourage a change in mindset. Some refuse to deviate from the path of conflict and quite often will ultimately leave. Many thrive, by embracing and adapting to positive change, whilst others become marginalised malcontents, simmering away in the background but mostly keeping their issues to themselves.

Conflict can also arise from a touch too much passion or enthusiasm. This is rarely a long-term problem and can be quickly overcome. If anything, it is a good problem to have. I have always said I would sooner have to rein in a team or individual than have to put my boot up their backside to get them going! If an over-zealous approach leads to some conflict, it usually falls more into the 'healthy tension' category described earlier.

One thing I have never subscribed to is when some managers or 'leaders' deliberately create conflict. This can be with a positive intent as a catalyst to spark creativity, but some even do it for their own amusement. (Hitler enjoyed having his acolytes squabbling for his favour!) I worked with someone whose team described how their boss would deliberately 'throw a hand grenade' into the team meetings because they liked to see what happened. Not a style I would support. Playing 'Devil's Advocate' and challenging ideas is constructive, but hand grenades were invented to hurt, maim and destroy. This seems more like a power game or ego trip than a way to build a team.

To be clear, I consider healthy tension to be constructive and very important. The 'Emperor's New Clothes' environment where everyone nods and won't say what is obvious is not the way forward. It leads to groupthink and stifles progress. Challenge is crucial but needs to avoid becoming conflict, remaining at a productive not destructive level.

Dealing with Conflict

The first step is to determine if conflict is driven by either behaviours *and* some principles or is genuinely just principle-based.

If the former, there is less likelihood of satisfactory outcomes. It is best to either delay or even avoid the conflict by closing it down (in a group environment) and working with those causing the conflict separately and in private. Try to find out the cause or reasons for the behaviours and coach the person or group to refrain, emphasising the damage they are doing. If they won't, you may need to keep them out of situations where they can create issues while you work on a longer-term solution, possibly in tandem with HR.

When conflict is purely principle-driven, it is vital to have the views aired, discussed, and considered, even if all do not agree. So long as they *all commit* to a way forward you can move on. You can only get to this if there is a high degree of trust between individuals or within a team. Only with trust can you successfully resolve conflict and move through the subsequent stages of Lencioni's model.

Final Thought

TRUST is such an important word in business. If you think you have it, but really you haven't, you may end up being stabbed in the back!

A few points to ponder

- **Appreciate that there is a relativity to conflict and seek to take an objective view.**

- **Understand who and what factors are causing disagreement.**

- **Determine whether the conflict is purely on principle or driven by behaviour and respond accordingly.**

CHAPTER 9

PANDORA'S BOX

Motivation

The principles of leading, managing and motivating others run right through this book. A few simple ideas have helped me manage the motivation and development of individuals in the teams I have managed. No complex psychological theories or models, just some basic guidelines:

- Listen to your people
- Know them, understand them and encourage them
- Celebrate their skills and successes
- Draw learning from their setbacks
- Support their development needs

As Aleksandr (Compare the) Meerkat would say, 'Simples.'

Networking

'If you want to get ahead, get a set of clubs' was some advice given to me early in my Procter & Gamble career after I'd told a colleague that I didn't play golf. The person giving the advice had only been in the business a year or so longer but had got to grips with the 'game' that had to be played. To be fair, they went on to have a hugely successful career and reached the highest levels in one of the biggest global FMCG companies, so early appreciation of the power of networking really paid off.

Of course, building relationships that matter within your organisation and externally is extremely important for a successful company and a blossoming career. It's the terminology that often causes discomfort. Building a broad and effective personal network requires a blend of personality, charisma and interpersonal skills. However, when 'network' was used as a verb in the FMCG world it portended a more cynical, exploitative and obsequious approach.

Whilst I have always been able to make friends and find connections with people, I'd typically say that I wasn't a particularly good networker in a business sense. I always feel a little disingenuous approaching someone because of what their role and position might be able to do for me, as opposed to who they are as a person. For others, small talk and making contacts is an innate skill. I have witnessed some smooth, effective operators, completely at ease with both CEO and the security person at the entrance. For me though, building effective networks takes time and requires a degree of familiarity and trust. If the relationship you develop isn't genuinely robust, resilient and reciprocal, you can open yourself to the accusation of merely being a 'namedropper'.

Networking away from FMCG has opened my eyes though. In the small to medium enterprise (SME) environment, it is a more facilitated and enjoyable activity. The events run by organisations like regional Chambers of Commerce, local business clubs and Business Network International (BNI) have been set up by like-minded people with like-minded objectives. They are structured and open to people developing referral partners and clients, rather than jostling with a hundred other suppliers for a minute in front of a buying director or CEO.

I enjoy the business breakfasts and networking sessions facilitated through my membership of St Helens, Halton and Greater Manchester Chambers. There are dedicated people there who are focused on championing their local business communities and providing valuable support to the local economy.

BNI tends to create polarised views due to how structured and orderly the events and meetings are. It is a truly global organisation with a great emphasis on training and personal development. I was impressed when on one of the training webinars the Procter & Gamble origin story was referred to. People tend to either love BNI or recoil from it. From my perspective, the chapter I engaged with had some great characters and successful people, however, I have committed my time to more local groups like Real 5 St Helens and the Orion Marketing Group in Wigan.

Know, Like, Trust

This is a phrase I have heard a lot in SME circles, though I've tended to summarise this through my career as the notions of *like* versus *respect*.

The people you tend to admire the most are the ones you like AND respect.

Some you may respect due to their technical skills performance, results etc., but you might not like them that much. Their style may be very different from your own.

Then there are people you like, whose company you might enjoy, but you don't always respect some of the things they do or their approach to certain situations.

Finally, at the bottom of the list are the people you neither like nor respect and you tend to avoid.

We meet and interact with a variety of people and sometimes how you view them changes for better or worse once you get to know them more. The biggest disappointment tends to be when someone's actions and behaviours, or a group you have liked and respected, starts to erode those feelings. It has happened to me a few times with senior people I've looked up to, or a group I've been part of, behaving in a way that resulted in me feeling a little duped, or even betrayed.

Meetings

During most business careers we spend a huge amount of our time in meetings of one form or another. Some are stimulating and enjoyable, while in others you can tell that most people would rather be somewhere else. Managing effective meetings is a skill that whole books have been written about and of course in 2020 pretty much the whole business community utilised virtual meetings. Many salespeople, in particular, were already familiar with Microsoft Teams and Google Hangouts but for many, Zooming was a new experience.

I shared this guidance with my team a long time ago, so long ago that I can't remember who to credit for some of the source material.

Whatever type of meeting you're leading, whether it's in-person or virtual, you'll have a better chance of being successful when the participants follow some general protocols and agree on the 'rules'.

Some rules are established and documented, while others simply constitute good manners. For example, if you're asked to attend a meeting, you acknowledge whether or not you'll be attending. You review the agenda. You arrive on time. If it's necessary to leave the meeting early, you let the leader know.

Most who attend meetings know that someone—usually the meeting leader—manages the agenda and time. Notes are taken during the meeting and distributed after. Participants don't 'talk over' one another, and when someone makes a comment, it's appropriate to acknowledge that it was heard, whether you agree with what was said or not.

In many companies, it's an acceptable protocol for a participant to call attention to time or agenda issues if the facilitator doesn't. When a subject occurs that is unrelated to the agenda or takes the meeting off course, participants generally agree that a 'car park' can be used to capture these for later discussion. Participants in virtual meetings generally agree that background noises are disruptive. This includes multi-processing such as checking emails or filing during the meeting. Whatever rules you establish for your meetings, make sure they promote the following:

- **Equality** - This prevents one or two people from dominating a meeting and preventing others from having the opportunity to speak. People must respect one another's opinions and ideas and allow them the chance to voice them.

- **Harmony** - Participants should not have to raise their voices or argue to be heard. When there are set rules as to when people may speak, you attain better harmony.

- **Efficiency** - If there are fewer problems during your meetings, you won›t waste time managing difficulties. Instead of spending time trying to get your meetings under control, you can spend it on accomplishing your objective.

It's important to establish ground rules. They'll help promote equality, harmony, and efficiency. They also provide a reference when issues occur later. If, for example, a participant is preventing others from speaking, it's appropriate to refer to the ground rules and remind participants that they agreed to allow everyone to speak.

This all sounds a bit formal but doesn't have to be. With trust, transparency and appropriate respect for others, a meeting can flow.

Digging

On many occasions, I have dealt with people who behave as if every situation has a right or wrong outcome and of course, they are always right! Whether such absolute conviction stems from arrogance or insecurity varies with the individual but it doesn't tend to be helpful, either with peers or in a position of authority. What is even worse is if that person sticks resolutely to their guns, becomes overly defensive and develops an entrenched position. Having dug themselves into a hole, they just keep on digging! A little bit of humility and a few acts of contrition can often have a disproportionately positive effect.

The Miner's Lamp

The analogy here is a tendency for some managers to operate wearing a miner's lamp on their head, which identifies and isolates both certain projects and/or certain individuals under intense light but leaves others in the dark, neglected. This can impact morale and motivation negatively and inhibit progress in other areas. Whilst some projects are of shorter duration, other projects end up viewed as the flavour of the month or a manager's hobbyhorse—the latter move on, but the people left behind who have invested a lot of time and effort feel forgotten or confused. In people management terms the phrase 'blue-eyed boy' or 'teacher's pet' is used by overlooked or resentful colleagues. When managers are perceived to have favourites who are always engaged to help with pressing issues or an ongoing priority (that is, where the miner's light is shining), they can be considered unfairly elevated in status. This can cause a degree of friction with their colleagues but can also leave the individual feeling a little insecure when they are not receiving as much attention.

Walk the Talk

This is a phrase I have heard often and it's all about commitment and being intentional in your thoughts and actions or 'doing what you say you'll do', to put it in simpler terms. In all walks of life, you encounter many people who talk the talk but don't walk it. This happens at all levels in organisations but is probably most damaging when senior figures neglect to lead by example. Actions often speak louder than words.

When all of Kellogg's senior managers were invited to attend the *Thinking Outside the Box* training (a sizeable investment), the day started with the MD spending five minutes extolling the virtues of the training and how important it was to the future of the business. Then he promptly buggered off and wasn't seen again across the two days!

When I was in the marketing team, we also had some training centred around the idea of *'mi casa, tu casa'* (my house, your house) and the importance of trying to see and understand things from another person's perspective. The training was good and made a lot of sense. In a meeting not long after, I asked the marketing director who had commissioned the training to see if he could try to consider something from my perspective. He flatly refused! So much for the twenty thousand pounds training! So much for 'walking the talk'.

The leadership programme in my latter days at Barr included all the department heads from the management board, plus various other senior managers and the executive directors who remained for the duration of the course. Whilst there might have been the odd suggestion of scepticism and a few obsequious remarks from those looking to impress, by attending the program and participating fully, the directors provided a great example of 'walking the talk'.

The first time I heard the phrase 'be tough on the problem, not the people' was regarding Tesco and I consider the sentiment very appropriate. I have never worked for Tesco, so I don't know whether this mantra is adhered to internally. Unfortunately, I have experienced situations across most of the grocery multiples and occasionally in wholesale when this has been distorted and pressure has been directed personally rather than on fixing the problem.

Self-perception

Some of the personality profiles and psychometric testing I have experienced address the differences between self-perception (how you see yourself) and how others perceive you. I am far from an expert in decoding all the data from the various tools and profiles used, so my observations here are brief.

One thing that does strike me is that some people get hung up on the word *perception* and the phrase *perception is reality*. Of course, we all make judgements and observations based on how we perceive people and situations, and as humans we all make mistakes. For example, I've heard many variations around the theme of 'I never really liked him, but once you get to know him, he's really sound' which illustrates how we can get things wrong. However, during my career, the people who I have witnessed to be most disgruntled by the word *perception* tend to be those with lower self-awareness and less propensity to be honest with themselves. Net result: their self-perception and others' perception of them are misaligned!

Self-proclaimed

In a similar vein, I have always been wary of those prone to self-proclamation. Of course, some are considered experts in their fields and really are, but it is typically others who bestow this title on them. If you are going to describe yourself as an expert in something, you had better be one! This does tend to rub against the grain in business. Just look at LinkedIn profiles where most of us feel the need to sell ourselves. One person I worked with for many years often referred to their own 'high-levels of integrity' and 'honest approach', effectively using these statements like a challenge. I found this passive- aggressive behaviour uncomfortable as they were almost daring you to question them. I had several altercations with them regarding their honesty and integrity. However, as this type of person will rarely make admissions, you must have incontrovertible evidence to 'call them out'.

Recruitment and Interviewing

I have interviewed hundreds of people throughout my career and it is typically an activity I enjoy. Sometimes you are won over by a person as soon as they enter the room whilst others you warm to and the liking gets stronger as the interview progresses. However, on some occasions, you realise straight away that they should never have been called in, to begin with!

Companies have different recruitment and interviewing strategies, and the process continues to evolve through online screening, profiling, interviews on Zoom and even interviews effectively conducted by robots where you are asked questions by a pre-filmed interviewer. However, I still hold to the adage that people do business with people. We possess emotions and instincts that we need to keep using.

The person who doesn't bother to turn up for an interview (as opposed to the person you occasionally come across who is there in body but not mind!) is always a frustration and the problem is usually the result of either bad planning or bad manners. There is also a flip side to this coin though. I was never particularly comfortable with the idea of benchmarking external candidates with your own personnel. In terms of comparing abilities when appointing someone to an actual role then fair enough. However, I have experienced scenarios where a company benchmarks to 'see what's out there' with no real intention to recruit or just to legitimise a preferred internal appointment. This is not a transparent activity and borders on arrogance when it wastes candidates' time.

Second Chance Saloon

Some of the world's great organisations have policies that mean once you have left, you can't come back. This was certainly the belief when I was at Procter & Gamble. When I did hand in my notice, it was primarily for geographical reasons. I had just got married, we had our first child on the horizon and so I wanted to stay in the North West. The sales VP was understanding and said some words that I have always appreciated. He said that in all his years with the company he had only ever met one person with such a strong geographical attachment as myself and that if things didn't work out with my move to Kellogg's, I should contact him and he would find a way to re-employ me. It was hard leaving such a first-class operation as Procter & Gamble and hearing those words made it even harder. I had looked to leave a few years before and had been persuaded to stay—one of the best decisions I ever made, but this time was different; I needed to move on.

Since then, I have always been prepared to let good people come back onto the team. For some, it is an ego issue in not wanting to let someone return. When I was making such decisions at AG Barr, I was purely focused on getting the best possible person for the job. If we did not have an appropriate candidate internally, I would recruit outside and on several occasions that meant the return of a prodigal. We all make mistakes, and my view is that if a really good operator has realised that the grass isn't greener on the other side, they could hit the ground running on their return and their gratitude would probably make them even more committed than previously. Clearly, you would not take just anyone back, but why penalise the person and the organisation if they were effective, popular and could add value?

If someone you already know is a strong performer, describes what you've built as 'a work culture with high trust levels, where everyone is valued', and admits that they 'knew from the moment [they] left that no other business can replicate this one'—and finally offers an 'I am extremely grateful that I was able to come back and I do owe you much more than a pint or two'—wouldn't you be pleased to welcome them back?

The Beliefs of Excellence

For the last twenty or so years, I have often referred to the seven *Beliefs of Excellence* by Cecara Consulting, introduced during my time with Kellogg's. They are simple ideas that provide resolute guidance.

1. Everyone is unique.
2. Everyone makes the best possible choice available to them at the time.
3. There is no failure, only feedback.
4. Behind every behaviour is a positive intention.
5. The meaning of the communication is the response that you get.
6. Mind and body are part of the same system.
7. The person with the most flexibility in thinking and behaviour stands the best chance of success.

Yes, some of the beliefs can be difficult to accept with specific individuals and in certain circumstances. However, I have always found them a great way to help me understand and appreciate the things I haven't readily agreed with.

A few points to ponder

- **Build and utilise an effective network but be wary of name dropping.**

- **'If you want to get ahead, get a set of clubs'—to be fair, this *can* help!**

- **Being liked and respected is a wonderful position to attain but remember the responsibility you carry. People feel duped and even betrayed if your standards slip.**

- **If you wear a miner's lamp, widen the beam.**

- **Walk the talk.**

- **Commendations, complements and positive feedback are infinitely more valuable when they come from others, not yourself.**

- **If a talented, sincere, and honest individual makes a mistake by leaving, why not let the prodigal return?**

'I remember the time you had recently joined, and we were on a training course. You came to partner me in an exercise, and I felt privileged to have a senior manager as I was the least experienced member of staff. This gave me confidence to carry on and not to give up on anything.'

Mukesh, Local Business Development Manager, Barr Soft Drinks.

'You have always been so friendly, approachable and "one of us". The way you engage an audience is inspiring. Thanks for giving me my first break into sales at the ripe old age of forty-something, a time when I really needed the confidence and financial boost.'

Debra, Business Development Executive, Barr Soft Drinks.

'I just want to say thankyou! I have worked with numerous senior leaders in business and within the RAF reserve forces and I can without doubt state you have been a true inspiration. I admire your strength in character when tough decisions need to be made, yet a genuine interest in subordinates. These are qualities which are often rare within one individual and this has made working for you a true pleasure.'

Aman, Business Development Manager, Barr Soft Drinks.

'Thank you for all that you have done to build Barr into what it is today— there was a small core of folk that came in when we were tiny and created something that others wanted to be a part of—you were key to this. You've been a consistently high-profile leader in the company with a huge following of admirers. You always look out for your people, always speak up for what is right and fair and always had time to share some advice and support. I hope that you are proud of all that you have achieved.'

Stuart, Finance Director, Barr Soft Drinks.

BUILDING BUSINESS: TALES FROM THE TRENCHES

CHAPTER 10
STRATEGY AND TACTICS

Strategy is the second prominent business word that I would often ask interviewees to define (the first being leadership). Answers would vary appreciably, and this is an area where scholars, analysts and others have spent a good deal more time in understanding than I have. I would never describe myself as a 'grand strategist' and at Procter & Gamble my personal development feedback often said I needed to demonstrate improved strategic thinking.

Ironically, on arrival at Kellogg's, I was soon advised that I needed to focus less on strategy and 'roll up my sleeves more' to get things done!

On one occasion, Carlos Gutierrez, the CEO, was over from the Battle Creek, Michigan head office for a management conference at the Bridgewater Hall in Manchester. When it came to the question and answer session the usual array of questions were asked (for example, 'If you could wave a magic wand to change anything in the business what would it be?', 'How important is new product development (NPD)?', etc.). Then someone asked Carlos about his strategy for long-term growth in the share price and company valuation. The answer was interesting—'if we keep hitting our sales numbers on a quarterly basis, investors will have confidence in our stock, and it will continue to rise'. This simple, short-term focused response took many by surprise when they were expecting some grandiose, intellectualised formula for growth.

In AG Barr, I consistently achieved the short-term deliverables (with customers) to hit the performance requirements in a UK plc, to then get feedback in my appraisal suggesting that I needed to expand my strategic thinking and focus farther ahead! Confused? Yes, so was I at times!

In considering the difference between strategy and tactics I found a light-hearted quote from Frank Muir, the celebrated writer, entertainer, and raconteur. It is rather old school and does demonstrate a degree of male chauvinism as he describes 'Strategy is buying a bottle of fine wine when you take a lady out for dinner. Tactics is getting her to drink it.'

I have seen *strategy* defined in various ways. One simple description is that strategy is the effort to align external opportunity with internal capability. Returning to Procter & Gamble, we were taught that strategy was the choices made to beat competition over the long term. They developed the cascading OGSM Model (objectives, goals, strategies and measures) which is an excellent, logical framework though I found that few had the time and inclination to rigorously ensure the update and intellectual integrity. I have since seen OGSM deployed elsewhere in adapted and diluted forms.

At one grocery conference, Mark Price (now Lord Price) made a presentation about strategy. He discussed the strategic effectiveness of doing the opposite of your competitors. So, when Tesco, Sainsbury's, etc., were pushing points-based, delayed-benefit loyalty card schemes, Waitrose offered their card holders a free coffee in their cafe on every store visit instead. This was incredibly successful in attracting customers to the stores, so much so, that they eventually had to change it due to abuse from free loaders!

Top businesses seek to recruit the brightest minds, however, Lord Price's observation is often overlooked when a 'monkey see, monkey do' reaction to competitive activity can take over. Early in the nineties

Procter & Gamble and Unilever had both looked to reduce packaging and save costs on laundry products by introducing plastic pouches to refill soap powder boxes. Procter & Gamble picked up intelligence that Lever Brothers had placed an order for literally hundreds of thousands of rectangular tin boxes. Putting two and two together they realised what Lever were probably trying to do. They sought an alternative supplier and ordered biscuit type tins branded as Ariel, Fairy, Daz and Bold and then sold them containing a refill pouch of the respective brand of powder. I honestly can't remember who got to shelf first, but the market was awash with them for months!

On a couple of occasions at AG Barr, we resisted the urge to just copy our rivals. Firstly, when concentrated energy drink shots were launched by Relentless and Red Bull and other brands responded, Rockstar had these products in the US and wanted to launch them. However, the AG Barr view was that they were not really soft drinks and declined. When Britvic launched Robinson's Squash'd small bottles of super concentrate for 'squash on the go', Vimto and some others followed suit. AG Barr were a minor player in the cordials and dilutes market though there were suggestions that we should launch something similar under the Simply brand. We didn't. Fortunately, common sense prevailed, as it is fair to say that both energy shots and Squash'd products burned dimly and briefly and could not be considered a success.

Boost Drinks have maintained a clear strategy that contrasts with most of their competitors in energy drinks. They chose to only supply the wholesale and independent retail channels, electing to not seek distribution of their products in the national grocery retailers. This approach has made them highly relevant to the customers they do work with and led to incredibly strong, close relationships. Whilst securing listings for their products in supermarkets could massively increase their volumes, Boost continue to operate to a strict, disciplined and successful strategy.

In the twilight of my career at AG Barr, the Soft Drinks Sugar Levy was announced and came into force in April 2018. There were two distinct strategies deployed: Coca-Cola, Britvic (Pepsi) and Red Bull maintained their original full-sugar variants in conjunction with existing sugar-free products. Lucozade and AG Barr chose to reformulate their products with reduced sugar versions of key brands to avoid the levy.

Although AG Barr comprehensively tested the reduced sugar IRN-BRU recipe with consumers and had the new products' acceptability confirmed by the completely independent *BBC One Show*, many consumers in Scotland were not happy. Campaigns to 'bring back IRN-BRU' were launched on Facebook and retailers who stockpiled the old full-sugar products ended up selling cans for up to eight pounds each! Despite the consumer backlash, AG Barr's board were reluctant to bring back full-sugar IRN-BRU. They introduced a full-sugar, high caffeine IRN-BRU Energy and then a Limited Edition 1901 style IRN-BRU after I had left but did not fully accede to consumers' wishes. However, in March 2021, they did announce that 1901 IRN-BRU would remain a permanent part of the range. Whilst this wasn't exactly what consumers wanted it is a gesture to meet part-way. It is possible for a brand to do a 'U-turn' with consumers and become even stronger, which you will read about in Chapter 16.

Having spent so long in FMCG, the concept of brand loyalty has always been salient, with various tools and measures to track and monitor it. In *Breaking Big* written by The Business Doctors, they make an interesting point. 'If you really believe that customers will stay loyal to your brand simply out of habit or comfort or personal loyalties, it's time to think again.'

Over the years I have witnessed the growth but also the demise of many brands. In some cases, I have been convinced that decline was due to excessive meddling by marketeers and brand managers wanting to leave their mark on a brand through new positioning, packaging changes or reformulation. Of course, we all accept that you cannot stand still in business, however, ego or ambition should never come before what is right for consumers.

When I started my career, launches of new product developments were few and far between, though the pace of development and launches of new products increased exponentially. The failure rate tends to be high and FMCG companies' profit and loss accounts often carry significant amounts for write-off costs. With the examples of energy shots and Squash'd, at least AG Barr avoided two of them!

Michael Porter of the Harvard Business School reflected both the Procter & Gamble and Lord Price approach when he said, 'Strategy is about making choices, trade-offs; it's about deliberately choosing to be different.'

You may recall, I never claimed to have great strategic insight. I am content to describe strategy loosely as the processes, plans and choices needed to bring about a desired future, such as achievement of a goal or solution to a problem, which requires effective planning and efficient marshalling of resources. Something like that anyway!

Or more succinctly, as I say to SMEs now, strategy is about making the right choices for growth. Tactics are the means by which a strategy is carried out, through planned and improvised activities to deal with current demands and deliver objectives supporting the longer-term goal. If anyone feels the need to improve on these definitions, I am certainly happy to be educated!

Finally, I have often considered the idea of a specific strategy document as something like a grail quest. Yes, sometimes a grand strategy is succinctly captured and shared around an organisation for all to consider, like a written constitution. However, often a strategy evolves and develops less formally, more like the UK's unwritten constitution than a sacred strategy scroll that can be held and cherished.

Budgets and Targets

There is one other important point to make about monitoring and measuring progress—an old adage that I've found invariably holds true. 'You get what you measure' or 'what gets measured gets done'.

There is a caveat though. This only works if the goals, targets and objectives are sensible, or SMART.

- Specific
- Measurable
- Achievable
- Relevant
- Timebound

When I started with Procter & Gamble, the acronym was SMAC, which stood for specific, measurable, achievable and compatible. The SMART version came later though the R was for Realistic. One of my colleagues at AG Barr suggested that *achievable* and *realistic* were effectively duplicates and proposed that the R should be for relevance. This was a great intervention as you will see in the next chapter.

Two examples highlight the importance of getting budgets and targets right, or SMART, specifically the A part.

The year 2018 was the hottest summer in the UK for over forty years, which of course was good news for the sales of soft drinks and ice cream. However, in July 2019, AG Barr issued their first ever profit warning and in an annual report for results ending in January 2020 the chairman wrote, 'Looking back, we did not fully recognise the extent to which we benefited from the hot summer of 2018. The budget set for 2019 was too optimistic versus the exceptional weather in the base.' Their 2019 budget was overly ambitious and unachievable. It was SMRT.

When I arrived at Flavour Warehouse one of my first tasks was to develop a sales budget for the next financial year, starting from December 2019. The new chief financial officer was not due to start for a couple of months and being inexperienced in the vaping category I consulted previous years' budgets and sought the input of the owner, head of sales and members of the finance team. The budget was approved, but over time I started to question the robustness of the assumptions. Certain parts of the business were not performing as well as initially suggested and the growth expectations made me uncomfortable. Vaping then became the centre of a negative media storm in the US, which had an impact on category performance. One month into the financial year I asked the question in a board meeting as to whether we should consider revising the budget expectations so that we would not spend a year of frustration and demotivation chasing numbers that were only *SMRT*. Unfortunately, there was no support for this idea.

I completely understand that it is not good practice to continually adjust a business's numbers, particularly in a listed company. 'Soft' or 'reduced' targets are not the recipe for aggressive and consistent growth, however, when budgets or targets are not **SMART** from the outset you are also unlikely to get the performance you aspire to.

I have always been as driven to hit my targets as any salesperson due to professional pride and not just because they were linked to bonuses and remuneration, but without budgets and targets that are SMART, despondency can spread right through the organisation

Again, there can be an element of 'greyness' here. 'You get what you measure' is a great principle but it depends on the accuracy of the measuring and having properly calibrated (SMART) benchmarks.

A few points to ponder

- *Strategy* and *leadership* are frequently used words in business but not everyone understands them.

- Meeting a competitor's strategy head on can often be appropriate so long as it isn't just 'monkey see, monkey do'.

- It takes courage and conviction to do the opposite of your competitors and there are no guarantees of success.

- Listen to consumers and do not be afraid to admit to a mistake.

- If objectives or goals are not SMART, people can (and will) switch off.

CHAPTER 11

R & R

I found this interesting quote from Kevin Roberts, CEO of Saatchi & Saatchi.

> *'Here is my equation for success on brands and business:*
> ***[IQ+EQ+TQ+BQ]CQ'***

(Translation: Intelligence, emotion, technology, bloody quick, with a creativity quotient.)

I really like Kevin's idea, though my path to success formula is a little simpler:

R + R = Growth

From my earliest days at Procter & Gamble I realised that successful outcomes were largely driven by the power of your brand and how productive your relationships were with your customers (that is, retailers and wholesalers). The latter would allow you to 'get products onto the shelf', whilst the former would ensure consumers or shoppers would 'take them off the shelf' and buy them.

Over time I refined my thinking to conclude that growth (or success on brands and business as in Kevin Roberts' description) was essentially down to R&R.

R&R can mean many things depending on the situation, though the first one that springs to mind (as per collinsdictionary.com) is in the military context of rest and recuperation. Alternatives include a medical R&R (rescue and resuscitation) and a leisure focused R&R (relaxation and recreation).

From my experience in business, R&R is the relevance of your proposition (to your customers and consumers) and the relationship you have with them.

Therefore, as depicted in the chart below:

$$Relevance + Relationship = Growth$$

R&R

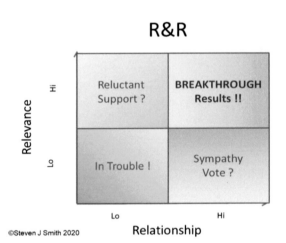

©Steven J Smith 2020

Business at RISK: If you have a weak proposition then you tend to be of low relevance to your customers. Plus, if your relationships are poor and unproductive, your business (if you have any) will always be at risk and unlikely to grow.

Reluctant SUPPORT: When relevance is high due to powerful branding, consumer understanding and high-profile marketing, or if you have more niche products with strong loyalty that deliver decent retailer profit, then even if relationships are not that great, your proposal is likely to be supported, albeit reluctantly. Strong market-leading companies (for example, Procter & Gamble and Kellogg's) often tend to be in this box.

Retail and wholesale customers may view the supplier as too controlling or even arrogant, however, as they are so good at what they do their shoppers will still demand the products. Not supporting them can put wider sales at risk. This was something we always leveraged on Pampers—it was the market leading nappy and the young families purchasing them were typically the highest spending shoppers. (NB: Customers sometimes referred disparagingly to Procter & Gamble people as 'Proctoids', suggesting that they were all similar men in grey suits who were brainwashed with process!)

One of the most sobering incidents and biggest learnings of my career came in a situation when I assumed a stronger relationship existed than I had. Even though the relevance of Barr's proposition to the customer was high, my mistake put the relationship and business with a customer on the line. Fifteen years on, I still replay the incident and run through how I could have avoided it. The customer was a large discount chain that the commercial director had typically managed himself through a direct relationship with the owner. I had been in the meeting where we had agreed on the year's plan, but a few months in, despite providing our agreed investment, the customer had only ordered a fraction of the sales agreed on. The CEO was worried and with my boss away on holiday, I picked up the phone.

After a friendly and cordial introduction, we danced around a business update but eventually I had to raise the current situation of sales being way behind the agreement. After a few non-committal assurances, I flippantly suggested that we 'weren't a charity' and needed to see a return on our investment. It was intended as a joke, but it certainly wasn't received that way! A torrent of expletives and threats to close the account boomed down the phone and I admit to being quite shaken by the reaction. I backpedalled furiously, apologised profusely and eventually the situation calmed down. I often referred to it with my own team as an example of over-playing a relationship and the story became something of a standing joke. The word *charity* was often used to put me in my place thereafter! Lesson learned big time—the meaning of the communication is the response you get.

SUPPORT without Substance: Sometimes individuals or even the whole company thrive on having great relationships with their customers even if ultimately their product or proposition is weak or irrelevant. Sometimes this may be due to a historical relationship between company founders or it may be that the supplier has over invested in key personal relationships. Alternatively, it could just be that certain individuals at a certain point in time really get on and like each other, so they do good business together. However, if the emphasis is based too much on relationship, it may not endure changes in personnel so the support may lack substance over time.

In the early eighties, Clive Sinclair had been the key driver of Margaret Thatcher's vision of a computer in every home ensuring Britain led the way in pioneering computer penetration. Through the ZX80, ZX81 and crucially the ZX Spectrum, Sinclair enabled Britain to have the highest household penetration of personal computers in the world and made Sinclair a household name. He had delivered an affordable, hugely relevant product and secured a strong relationship with games-mad teenagers and parents who genuinely believed that the Spectrum would enhance their education!

Unfortunately, Clive Sinclair's other great intervention did not enjoy the same respect and became an object of ridicule. Just as the Spectrum was a pioneer of home computing, the Sinclair C5 was to pioneer a new era of greener, electric personal transportation; a concept way in advance of Elon Musk and Tesla. However, the C5 could only be described as a failure that destroyed Sir Clive's reputation.

Why?

Despite having built such an outstanding reputation and relationships as an inventor and computing pioneer, and whilst the concept of electric personal transportation was relevant in an era of rising oil prices, the actual proposition of the C5 was fundamentally flawed. A lightweight electric vehicle powered by a washing machine motor that could travel neither far, nor fast and accommodated the driver in a low horizontal position was extremely vulnerable and insecure on the open road. Production problems, battery problems and a comical appearance on the odd occasion they were seen in public resulted in a total disaster. Sinclair had good relationships and a positive reputation, but his proposition for changing commuter travel lacked true relevance.

Now we have electric assisted bicycles, scooters and of course Tesla have pioneered the fully electric car. By 2035, the government wants an end to production of internal combustion engine (ICE) vehicles and for all forms of transport to be fully electric. The electric transportation concept of the C5 is now hugely relevant, with current propositions getting stronger and stronger. Even so, it takes new entrants to the field a lot of time and investment to develop relationships and reputation. Tesla didn't make a profit in fifteen years.

BREAKTHROUGH RESULTS: What can be achieved when relevance and propositions are strong and the relationships even stronger?

When I joined the company, around three-quarters of AG Barr's revenue came from IRN-BRU and a similar proportion of sales came from Scotland, where five million Scots drink one hundred and fifty million litres of IRN-BRU a year, or thereabouts. The rest of the UK was almost considered as an export market, with only a small amount of business in London and the south. The soft drinks market still retains considerable geographic differences in the products consumed and the joke at the time was that Barr's business mirrored Bonnie Prince Charlie's advance—it petered out at Derby!

Being based in London with a predominantly southern footprint for their depots, Bestway's business with AG Barr was quite small. Relationships were good, but relevance was low. That all changed dramatically following two significant acquisitions and a new partnership in the mid noughties. Bestway acquired the Batleys' group whose cash & carry heartland was the north of England and Scotland. AG Barr then agreed to launch US energy drink brand Rockstar in the UK. Rockstar sponsored the high-profile boxing bout between Ricky Hatton and Floyd Mayweather providing an opportunity to showcase the brand by taking key customers, including Sir Anwar Pervez, the Bestway chairman, to Las Vegas to watch the fight. The following year, AG Barr bought the exotic juice brand Rubicon, the drink of choice for British Asian consumers and, aside from Coca Cola, the key soft drink sold through Bestway's cash & carry estate.

The mutual business soon became much more relevant for both parties as AG Barr had the key soft drink in Scotland with IRN-BRU (Scotland's other national drink) and in the London and south-east markets with Rubicon. Bestway now had cash & carries all across Great Britain. This was the start of a great business relationship that developed Bestway into AG Barr's biggest customer, even ahead of Tesco, and AG Barr became the second biggest soft drinks supplier to Bestway, behind only Coca Cola.

A strong 'top to top' relationship where the CEOs would join the sales and buying teams to align annual business plans filtered down to even stronger relationships within individual Bestway and Batleys' cash & carry depots. Barr's commercial director had a love of cricket matched by many within the Bestway team, so as the Rubicon brand started to get involved with cricket sponsorship there became a mutual passion added to the mix. I was never good enough to participate personally, however, an annual Bestway versus Barr cricket match became a hotly contested event.

A unique business incentive programme was agreed upon where the top-performing branches would be rewarded by Barr hosting a trip to see the Cricket World Cup in Barbados. This was incredibly successful in terms of mutual sales and became a regular feature, eagerly anticipated by the Bestway team. The trip included an educational element to study local developments in soft drinks and, naturally, had to be captured on AG Barr's corporate 'Risk, Hospitality and Bribery Register'. Other suppliers have tried to run similar activities with their customers but what set the Bestway/Barr approach apart was the genuine camaraderie. Whilst free time was available, we typically ate together and attended activities and sight-seeing as a full group with genuine friendships developing. In fact, one of the senior executives in Bestway commented that on many employees' desks, next to photos of their families, pride of place went to photographs from AG Barr trips!

Travelling to one of the events in 2016, I was seated in business class (only my second time ever—the first was a lucky upgrade!) on a BA flight to Las Vegas, with the then managing director, Martin Race. Martin is a straight-talking and down-to-earth leader, who earned great respect over a long career in wholesale. He has become a great friend and mentor and is *always* transparent and trustworthy. I related to Martin that my first experience of Bestway/Batleys was the grumpy old buyer in Liverpool and I never imagined that one day I'd be sharing a beer with the MD on route to the fun capital of the world!

AG Barr were awarded Bestway Supplier of the Year Award (as voted for by Bestway personnel) six times, at one point winning for three years consecutively. The business grew exponentially and illustrates the breakthrough that is possible when you have a **highly relevant** proposition, combined with an exceedingly **strong relationship**.

A few points to ponder

- Be sure of your relationship before you relax.

- When it comes to the crunch, Relevance trumps Relationship.

$$R + R = \nearrow$$

CHAPTER 12

SOOTY SAYS *NO!*

The lion's share of my career has been selling and negotiating with customers, or more specifically, spending hours of analysis, thinking and preparation time before meeting with them. Old adages and acronyms like the seven P's (Proper Preparation and Planning Prevents Piss Poor Presentation) and PSF (Persuasive Selling Format) spring to mind. There is a plethora of training companies and consultants (many with similar FMCG backgrounds to myself) who have become specialists in the field and I have worked with many of them over time. Most claim that theirs is the definitive and most successful approach, but reality tells me that results often come from the hybrid model of their teaching and your own experience.

As a manager and team leader, there are times when you simply have to be there for your people. No matter how confident or experienced someone is, in business there is always the possibility of facing a completely new and challenging situation. Support and togetherness are crucial at times and a sales career, in particular, can deliver great rushes of satisfaction but also exposure to confidence-crushing and at times humiliating outcomes.

In Netflix's *The Pharmacist*, Chris Davis, the former Purdue Pharma sales rep, describes how, as the negative PR around Oxycontin started to build, doctors would take his presentation or sales aid and just drop it straight into the bin. People face difficult scenarios in business and in all walks of life generally, but salespeople often face pretty blunt rejection. They sometimes need supporting, picking up and reassuring as well as being given tools to help them learn and benefit from their difficult experiences.

Before Aldi and Lidl came to UK shores, the flag bearer for discount grocery in the UK had been Kwik Save, which was established in north Wales in the late sixties. Kwik Save prospered by selling basic brands, straight from their cardboard boxes, in no-frills stores with narrow aisles and wooden shelves—a unique, low cost, limited line operating model with huge success in Wales, the north of England and ultimately nationally. It floated on the stock exchange in 1970 and by the mid-1990s had more than a thousand outlets.

When I managed Kwik Save for Procter & Gamble in the early nineties, they were challenging and aggressive to do business with, but it was a great time to work with them. They continued to grow sales and market share and could also be great fun. In face-to-face meetings, one of the buyers had a habit of breaking off from my presentation to suddenly dial up another supplier on speaker phone, making various demands, threats to de-list products and essentially bullying them. Hesitant at first, I used to sit there, twiddle my thumbs, and wait for him to turn back to me. Eventually, I told my manager what was happening and that I was struggling to deliver my presentations and hold his attention. Of course, my boss realised he was just trying to unsettle me and suggested I needed to fight fire with fire. After that I would go to meetings with a newspaper or a novel in my briefcase. When he started making calls I would sit back and read. After a while I was able to maintain his focus on what I was presenting.

You can view the buyer's behaviour as downright rude or just playing the game. If the latter, then he had learned from the master. The myths about some of Kwik Save's trading director's early tactics were legendary!

Major suppliers could not have envisaged that Kwik Save would eventually become a FTSE 100 Company with circa seven per cent shares of UK groceries. So early on, relatively junior sales managers would be sent to Prestatyn to deal with this small, idiosyncratic customer. The buying team became frustrated that the people they dealt with did not have the experience and authority to negotiate directly and make decisions face-to-face. Whether the following stories ever happened I do not know but given my experiences above it seems likely that there would be no smoke without fire even if there has been a degree of embellishment over the years.

In one story, when faced with a sales representative who could not, or would not, make a decision on a promotional investment or a request for improved pricing, the buying director would slide open a drawer in his desk and remove a large pair of scissors. He would then lean across the desk, grab the salesman's tie and cut it off halfway down (all FMCG business was conducted in suits, shirts and ties in those days—some companies even insisted on bowler hats or trilbies until the sixties!). The person would then be told to leave the premises and advise their superiors to send someone with the authority to negotiate next time!

On another occasion, a salesman from a drinks company was presenting a new product and encouraged the buying director to try the product as part of the sales pitch. He said he did not need to try it himself to know whether it could be a sales success, but the seller was insistent. 'Okay, I'll drink your product if you have a drink from me,' the buyer conceded. After trying the new product, he produced a bottle of whisky from his drawer, filled a large tumbler and insisted the salesperson honour their pledge. He was then told that three measures would take at least six hours to wear off and if seen driving his car beforehand he would be reported to the police!

Probably the funniest and perhaps most humiliating of the Kwik Save stories is when the eager salesman turns up, starts presenting and is suddenly told to stop. 'Why do you keep looking at me when you should be presenting to Sooty?' the salesman is asked as a Sooty glove puppet pops up from behind the desk and waves. 'Sooty is doing the buying today,' the buyer said and proceeded to insist that the rest of the presentation be directed at Sooty. At the end, Sooty whispers in the buyer's ear, he turns to the salesman and says, 'Sooty says we are not going to stock your product.'

If any of the above scenarios truly happened, how low would the salesperson have felt? Maybe, just maybe, the most experienced and thick-skinned could have laughed it off, but how do you explain it all to your boss and how would they deal with it? I once used a similar technique in a role play with a younger, less experienced, but uber-confident member of the sales team. They were nearly in tears and that was only at an internal meeting! A few colleagues told me I was wrong to do it and maybe they were right, but it's better to take someone down a peg or two in a safe environment than leave it to a real-life situation.

Whether Sooty ever did say no, whilst I was with AG Barr, we faced an even more challenging situation with a customer. It gained quite a lot of publicity and contributed to the eventual introduction of a UK Grocery Code Adjudicator and the Grocery Supply Code of Practice (GSCOP). As you shall see in the next chapter, I had to draw on the ancient art/ science of alchemy to get the right results.

A few points to ponder

- *No* doesn't always mean *no*—you just haven't made the proposition attractive enough to obtain a *yes*!

- Find a way to handle rejections and learn from disappointment. Do not just accept them.

- Aggressive behaviour in business is rarely personal, it is usually just a tactic.

CHAPTER 13

ALCHEMY

A university and Procter & Gamble colleague Jonathan Brown published a book in 2013 called *Stress and Success—Fast Fixes for Turbulent Times*. Having shared the script upfront, Jonathan asked if I would add a testimonial at the start. In doing so I referred to ancient alchemy and the quest to transform lead into gold, comparing it to Jonathan's aim to turn stress into an advantage. Looking back at my career, I can see alchemy as a very appropriate metaphor when difficult and dire situations have been worked into successful outcomes.

Soap Wars Part One

Procter & Gamble and Unilever were often considered to have created a duopoly in many home cleaning categories like laundry and dish-care. It was not a true duopoly as there were of course several other suppliers to the market (though retailers' own store brands had not taken off at this time). In the early nineties, Unilever fired a massive broadside at Procter & Gamble when they launched Persil washing up liquid to rival Procter & Gamble's Fairy, which was market leader by some distance. Persil was heavily backed with promotions, special offers and a heavyweight TV campaign featuring comedian Robbie Coltrane (pre his role as Hagrid in *Harry Potter*). They secured good levels of distribution in the grocery multiples who were always keen to back a credible challenger to a market leader, lessening their strength and influence.

Procter & Gamble had to act fast and decisively to defend Fairy Liquid. Persil was a challenger like none before and a massive investment in a UK defence plan was agreed. Procter & Gamble had become aware of Unilever's plans before Persil was on sale and wanted to get consumers to buy extra Fairy and 'pantry load' during Persil's initial trial period. This was before most stores had scanning facilities or the ability to do multi-buys and buy-one-get-one-free (BOGOF) promotions. Therefore, Procter & Gamble committed to producing huge quantities of twin packs with two bottles banded together for a special price. On the smaller five hundred millilitre-sized bottle there was a modest twenty-five per cent price reduction, but on the one litre there was an unprecedented deal of two for the price of one! Two litres of Fairy Liquid would take most families out of the market for months.

Even though the retailers were keen to support Persil, they could not refuse the strength of this offer, so Procter & Gamble had to allocate stock based on the customers' previous sales of the packs. For most this was fine, but with Kwik Save there was a problem. Being the original limited line discounter with a maximum of circa of two thousand, five hundred products in any store, Kwik Save only listed five hundred millilitres Fairy Liquid in original and lemon variants (two SKUs), and hence were not given an allocation of the one litre BOGOF pack. On hearing this news, the trading director went ballistic threatening all kinds of sanctions against Procter & Gamble's range as they simply couldn't be without the best value pack. This would be a disaster for them in the eyes of consumers who shopped in Kwik Save for the permanently low prices and best value around.

At one point the outlook was grim. Kwik Save stopped ordering Fairy Liquid and was warning of other consequences. Their stores attracted millions of shoppers a week, so it was an unacceptable situation for Procter & Gamble too. A creative solution was desperately required and my manager at the time (Mr Baked Alaska) provided it. Procter & Gamble would transfer Kwik Save's five hundred millilitre twin pack allocation to other customers and produce a new once-off amount of one litre BOGOF just for Kwik Save, who would also commit to listing original and lemon Fairy one litre ongoing. From having no Fairy Liquid in Kwik Save and a shattered relationship, Procter & Gamble then ended up with four SKUs and huge displays in-store. I looked on this as business alchemy transforming a grim, lead-like situation into glittering, shining gold. A lesson I would never forget.

These were the principles I employed in 2008 when pre-GSCOP, Tesco put huge pressure on the supplier base for better terms, increased investment and improved pricing. Tesco's approach through brief, timetabled, simultaneous sessions with suppliers caused outrage and upset at the time. I approached it differently and took the learnings from Kwik Save to look at turning a potentially very damaging situation into a way of building the business in the future—as I now explain.

Discounter House: Be Afraid, Be Very Afraid

In the autumn of 2008, Tesco sent a massive shudder through the supplier base. Competition in UK groceries had 'hotted up' and ultimately prompted headlines like 'Tesco posts worst figures in sixteen years' (The Observer). Rejuvenated competition from the likes of Asda and Sainsbury's plus the growing strength of Aldi and Lidl triggered a Tesco initiative that had suppliers furious and writing to The Grocer in despair at the retailer's brutal tactics. Articles also appeared in the mainstream national press.

My sales controller had been invited to a meeting with Tesco and I expected a debrief later in the day. I was surprised when he called literally fifteen minutes after the scheduled appointment. I was also concerned as I detected a tremor in his voice. My immediate thought was a car crash or some incident on route to Tesco Head Office in Cheshunt, but he explained that he had already been in and had the meeting. On arrival at Tesco House, the usual meeting location, he had been re-directed to a new meeting facility just down the road, called Discounter House.

Discounter House was a large building that had been fitted out like a prison waiting room (if TV depictions are accurate!) with sparse furnishings and a series of open cubicles for one-to-one discussions with suppliers. Posters and point of sale materials describing Tesco as Britain's biggest discounter adorned the walls, and displays had been built of a series of price fighter brands in key categories that were unique to Tesco. All very unusual and somewhat austere.

On sitting down in a cubicle with a buyer, with a dozen or so other suppliers in separate cubicles, my sales controller was presented with a single sheet of paper. This contained a brief summary of AG Barr's trading performance with Tesco, a request for improved pricing, increased promotional investment and a list of products that would no longer be ordered if everything wasn't agreed to within a week.

My first job was to provide comfort and reassurance to the controller. He was genuinely shaken as he had not managed the Tesco account for long and could see our business being decimated. Next, I had to think objectively and rationally about the situation as it was approaching the company's financial year end and could have a major impact on our overall results. Stephen Covey's rattlesnake analogy from *The Seven Habits* came to mind, so rather than be angry or indignant like many suppliers, I tried to relax and think about how we could turn this damaging situation into something positive.

As a relatively small supplier to Tesco with most of our strength in the north, we'd typically found it difficult to secure Tesco support for our brands other than IRN-BRU (Scotland was claimed to be one of only two markets where Coca Cola isn't the unequivocal number one in soft drinks). With other larger suppliers likely to fight Tesco with tooth and nail and, given they needed something from us, I persuaded our understandably concerned board that if we met some of their requests quickly, we could be in a unique position to not just save products from de-list but go on the 'front foot' and request more support for our wider portfolio.

We followed this strategy through a series of meetings and follow-ups where I always ensured that I was on hand to support the sales controller. On one occasion I thanked the Tesco team for setting up Discounter House and commended it as a great opportunity for suppliers—I am not sure whether they took me seriously or not. In December, *The Telegraph* ran an article about Discounter House with quotes from suppliers about 'outrageous' and 'amoral' demands and concerns that Tesco would drive suppliers out of business.

Discounter House in 2008 was a shock to the grocery system, but by keeping an open mind, evaluating it as an opportunity and working as a team, we truly turned a leaden situation into a golden outcome. Our sales revenue with Tesco nearly doubled over the next twelve months and continued to return strong and consistent growth thereafter.

Surfers and Swimmers

Other customers had similar investment objectives to Tesco although went about it in different ways. Morrisons called suppliers in for a series of presentations where they shared that they had two different views of suppliers. Some were positively designated as 'swimmers' because they put the effort in, worked hard with Morrisons and shared in mutual growth. 'Surfers' on the other hand enjoyed being carried along by Morrisons' progress without investing money or energy of their own. The follow up discussions were naturally quite different depending on how you were viewed as a supplier, and it is quite possible that another category may have been introduced: 'drowned'!

Perhaps the most impressive approach to this type of interaction from my perspective was Booker Wholesale. Suppliers would be invited to one of their cash & carry branches where after tea, coffee and snacks, CEO Charles Wilson (one of the most impressive and sincere people in the industry and another Procter & Gamble alumni) would deliver a business update highlighting Booker's consistent growth and performance. Smaller groups would then be led by Booker personnel onto the shop floor and walked around to a series of quick presentations on various product categories and Booker's business plans. Then it was back for a summary presentation and Q&A with Charles and the trading team. Afterwards, you were given a letter outlining Booker's (investment) 'ask' and the negotiations would begin. A much more refined and civilised approach than the bleakness of Discounter House!

The Breaking Point

One day I received a call from Tesco that was straight to the point. I was told that Tesco had a performance gap that it was looking to suppliers to fill. The soft drinks category had a target and within soft drinks, Barr was expected to provide a certain value of support. I dusted down my 'alchemy instruction book' and suggested to Tesco what we should expect to get in return. An agreement was eventually reached, although it was not as beneficial as in 2008. In fact, we were in dispute for quite some time with Tesco as to whether they had delivered what they had 'agreed' to.

In 2014, Dave Lewis took up the reins as Tesco CEO and what followed catapulted Tesco to the front pages—a 263 million pounds accounting scandal in over-stated profits and a subsequent fraud case. Christine Tacon had been named as the UK's first Grocery Code Adjudicator (GCA) the year before, which was described by consumer and competition minister Jo Swinson as 'an incredibly important position in the retail groceries sector making sure that large supermarkets treat their suppliers fairly and lawfully'. This brought the GCA and GSCOP into a much higher profile. The grocery industry and the behaviour of both suppliers and retailers had to change.

For a while, it was 'open house' on Tesco with the written media and even *BBC Panorama* investigating Tesco in 2015 and reporting how they 'turned the screw' on their suppliers as they struggled to deliver sales growth. Personally, I have myself experienced some rude, discourteous, and even quite insulting behaviours from Tesco personnel. In the *Panorama* programme my former Procter & Gamble colleague David Sables, now CEO of Sentinel Management Consultants, was interviewed and said that 'bullying was going on in highly pressurised environments with threats' and Tesco were 'extremely aggressive'.

This also needs putting into perspective though. I have worked with some incredibly talented and decent people at Tesco and we British do have a tendency to knock our own. On an individual level and perhaps even as policy, they undoubtedly 'crossed the line' regularly but Tesco are an incredible success story overall and one of the leaders in global retail. Jamie Oliver gained a lot of plaudits for his campaign against obesity and pushed hard for the UK Soft Drinks Sugar Levy to be introduced in 2018. However, credit should go to the initiative and product ranging strategy of then Tesco soft drinks buying manager, David Beardmore. By focusing on low sugar products, David removed so many calories from the nation's diet that he probably deserves an MBE!

Negotiation

There are many training providers and books on negotiation. Clearly, the more effective you are, the more you can deliver for your organisation or for yourself (in a domestic situation). It is a fascinating subject and should be a core competency for most people in business. When it comes to the big, strategic negotiations it pays to think big and not be afraid! Consider the idea of shifting paradigms and do not be constrained. A big request means an opportunity to reciprocate with an equally big expectation, before the process flows to an outcome.

On one training programme I attended, a lot of attention was given to 'opening extreme' in negotiation with a big request that is highly unlikely to be agreed to. To an extent this worked for us in Discounter House, but you have to be careful that you don't undermine your own credibility from the start. When elected as JCR president at university, one of my roles was to negotiate with the warden of the hall of residence over the time for last orders in the bar. It was a residents' licence like a hotel and in theory could have served twenty-four hours. At my first hall event after election, I was keen to impress those who had voted for me so I approached the warden about a bar extension. 'What time are you thinking?' he asked. His reply to my 3 am request was 'don't be so absurd—twelve o'clock, no later' and walked off.

In a kind of reverse scenario, I utilised this after a summon to see Sainsbury's. They had requested a level of investment from Kellogg's that was not only ridiculously extreme, but they were offering nothing at all in return. Even though it was not his style, the senior buyer started the meeting with very bullish demands that we agree to the investment 'or else….' My response was to say, 'Or what? Am I going to find a horse's head in my bed?' a reference to *The Godfather* film. There were four people in the room. It went noticeably quiet and then we all burst out laughing. The ice was broken and eventually we had a productive meeting.

On another occasion, I became frustrated during a one-way exchange with Tesco where my contact kept talking over me and would not let me complete a full sentence. In comic desperation, I raised up my arms and boomed out that the 'Great Tesco has spoken', mimicking when Dorothy and her gang finally got to meet the Wizard of Oz. For a few moments I thought I had gone too far that time, but eventually their tone softened and we had more of a two-way discussion.

The Equalizer

When we had more limited TV choices in the 1980s, one programme I enjoyed was *The Equalizer*. The series was later turned into a film with Denzel Washington. In the original, tough-guy actor Edward Woodward played a retired intelligence agent with a mysterious past, who used the skills from his former career to exact justice on behalf of innocent people who were trapped in dangerous circumstances. Woodward was Robert McCall (American mum, British dad) and oozed style with a high-end apartment, cruising around in a Jaguar XJ6 and sporting a classic trench coat. Essentially, he was a vigilante in New York City turning the tide on various villains and organised crime.

To enlist The Equalizer's support, people responded to a newspaper advertisement (no internet in those days of course).

'Got a problem? Odds against you? Call the Equalizer: 212 555 4200.'

During tough, tense negotiations with retailers, I bet many would have loved to have brought in Robert McCall to hand out some tough justice! In reality, that role has already been assumed by various training companies and management consultants. You now contact the likes of Dave Sables at Sentinel through their website rather than a classified advert in a newspaper.

This brings me on to an old joke:

Why does Edward Woodward have so many letter 'D's in his name?

Answer: because without them he would be Ewar Woowar, which just sounds silly.

If we didn't have the letter 'C', in the business world we'd find ourselves in a similar dilemma to Ewar Woowar. Think about how many key words and their derivatives beginning with C we use in work conversations every single day.

- Corporate, Company, Commercial
- Customer, Consumer, Competitor
- Calculation, Collaboration, Communication
- Consultation, Credibility, Choices
- Co-operation, Colleagues, Co-efficient,
- Coordination, Confidence, Conviction
- Creativity, Champion, Cash & Carry, etc.

A poignant point is that the letter C has a pivotal role regarding the crucial area of transparency discussed in Chapter 7 (for example, communication, consultation, collaboration, etc.).

However, with no letter C, all planning would be overt (instead of covert) and hence fully visible to all stakeholders, partners, and rivals alike. Maybe that level of transparency would lead us to the economists' nirvana of 'perfect competition' (without the C of course!).

(Definition and meaning: Perfect competition, also known as pure competition or a perfect market, is the market economy at its finest, the most open (transparent) and competitive market possible, a market where there are no monopolies, duopolies, oligopolies, oligopsonies or monopsonies).

Soap Wars Part Two

Before moving on, another duel between Procter & Gamble and Unilever is worth a mention. In the constant quest for the perfect laundry product, they were continually looking to upstage each other with new formulations, new dosing regimens, liquids, powders, gels and compact products.

In 1994, Unilever launched Persil Power to gain the upper hand on Procter & Gamble's flagship laundry brand Ariel. It then kicked off like never before in a somewhat comical fashion, though billions of pounds were at stake. Procter & Gamble bombarded journalists across Europe with coloured photographs of tattered rags washed in Persil Power detergent next to pristine garments laundered with Ariel. Procter & Gamble also commissioned lab tests showing how Unilever's Power detergent damaged clothes. They didn't just confine attacks to public relations; they also ran full-page newspaper adverts developed by Saatchi & Saatchi claiming that Persil Power 'rotted underpants' and condemning the brand. Even for those of us working in Procter & Gamble this was a bold and unprecedented step that took us all by surprise—and caused a few giggles too. Remember the phrase about not washing your dirty linen in public?

Unilever, which spent one hundred million pounds over five years developing Persil Power, vehemently denied the accusation, taking out full-page newspaper advertisements to get its own message across.

The Independent reported on the soap wars in June 1994. They showed a pair of Marks & Spencer's boxer shorts at the centre of the dispute that Procter & Gamble said it had washed sixteen times using its own Ariel Ultra—while washing an identical pair using the opposition's Persil Power. The allegation made was that Persil Power reduced the undies to a tattered state!

In January 1995, Sainsbury's and Waitrose, two of Britain's largest supermarket groups, removed Persil Power from their shelves following a similar announcement by Tesco, which said it was phasing out the detergent and replacing it with Persil New Generation, a detergent soon due for launch by Lever Brothers. Eventually, a few years later in a relatively low-key presentation, a Unilever executive admitted the issues with Persil Power. Now the launch is remembered as one of the great marketing fiascos.

A few points to ponder

- **Humour does have a place in business—it is about judging where and when to use it.**

- **Be bold but not foolish in negotiation.**

- **Open extreme but not so extreme that it puts credibility at risk.**

- **Utilise all resources available and never be afraid to call for help from an Equalizer.**

- **In tough situations, think of the ancient art of alchemy. How can you turn lead into gold?**

CHAPTER 14

SCALEXTRIC

I have always had a passion for keeping life simple, for example, limiting my use of social media to a few key applications so I don't get confused! I view business in a similar way. Allan Leighton, former CEO of Asda and chairman of the Co-operative, was the first person I heard quote that 'simplicity is divinity'. Also, I've never heard of a new CEO going into a business with a strategy to make it more complicated!

Certainly, the operations directors I worked with in FMCG would prefer a business model like a Scalextric racing set. You set up the track into a circuit and race the cars around as fast as you can. Occasionally they come off (all production lines need downtime and inevitably you get the odd breakdown) but essentially, it's a very simple concept. Whilst it is quite straightforward to apply this analogy to the operations and manufacturing within a business, it is a cerebral concept that can impact individuals across the *whole* organisation.

The more categories, products, brands, and individual SKUs in a business, manufactured across multiple production sites, coupled with broad-ranging consumer communication and marketing activities, plus various levels of pricing and promotional strategies, products subject to VAT or VAT exempt, plus other government rules and regulations on where products can be sold and to whom, the more pressure on peoples' mental 'bandwidth' (just like this long sentence).

Over time businesses grow 'arms and legs' and branch out into different sectors and markets. Clearly, there are many cases of diversification being part of a robust and effective strategy. When markets mature and growth becomes difficult, businesses can continue to grow and evolve by launching into different product categories.

Various products throughout history have also been developed as by-products from the manufacturing of other goods. Wright's Coal Tar Soap was developed by William Valentine Wright in 1860 from 'liquor carbonis detergens', the liquid by-product of the distillation of coal to make coke; the liquid was made into an antiseptic soap for the treatment of skin diseases.

Many companies have expanded from their product origins into linked or adjacent categories. Procter & Gamble started as candle makers and now operate in scores of household goods' markets, from laundry products and nappies to cosmetics. Historically, Procter & Gamble were also manufacturers of hot beverages and snacks. Kellogg's cornflakes were developed by Dr John Harvey Kellogg (an interesting and somewhat controversial character that readers can Google) at his Battle Creek, Michigan sanitorium as a medicinal product. His brother Will Keith was the business brain behind the Kellogg Company, which now operates in various food and snack categories such as Pringles, which they bought from Procter & Gamble for 2.7 billion dollars. Barr Soft Drinks started out as a cork cutter supplying stopper corks for glass bottles before moving into the manufacture of the soft drinks themselves.

Corporate branding, such as Kellogg's, Nestlé or Unilever, provides trust and credibility to individual brands like Nescafé or Persil that fall into the next level of the brand hierarchy. Often companies decide to launch into other categories by bouncing an existing, trusted brand name. For example, the Cadbury brands' core business is chocolate confectionary, however, the chocolate itself and Cadbury name is licenced to manufacturers in other categories such as drinks, cakes, ice cream and desserts. When Kraft bought Cadbury to form a new business, Mondelez, they bounced the Cadbury name across to a variant of Kraft Philadelphia cream cheese. Caterpillar is the US equivalent of JCB specialising in heavy machinery, such as bulldozers, but consumers can also buy Cat-branded footwear.

When such expansion is part of a well-researched and logical strategy then all is usually well and good and adds to the organisation's value. A multi-category business like Unilever may have the equivalent of twenty Scalextric tracks all running at once, the point being that they are still, in operational and cerebral terms, relatively straightforward.

In some cases, though, there can appear to be little link or logic to the collection of enterprises. For example, Tomkins group used to be known as the 'buns to guns' group as this was the diverse nature of their businesses owned, from Hovis bread to Mr Kipling cakes and Smith & Wesson handguns.

For a variety of reasons, some businesses develop into more of a Hornby train set. In common with Scalextric, the trains have a central circuit, but the layout becomes more and more complicated as points, sidings, branch lines, tunnels, signals, level crossings and turntables are added. The passenger trains are required to stop at stations and must be closely co-ordinated, so they don't crash into freight trains. The whole system is more complex and hence much slower and more susceptible to breakdown. In the diagrams, the two-car Scalextric layout is much simpler than the Hornby train system.

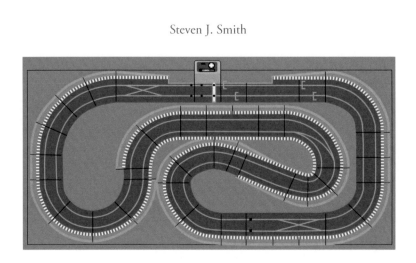

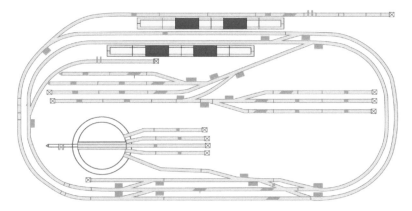

This point is reinforced in General Stanley McChrystal's *Team of Teams*, showing how organisations can stray from being complicated to being complex, which results in blurred focus, inefficiency and ultimately reduced effectiveness.

Why Does This Happen?

There can be many causes. From my experience, it is when a business is run more by 'personality than process'. Procter & Gamble was a business with very strong and established processes. Individuals tweaked and evolved the processes overtime. Essentially, people come and go moving on to other roles and assignments, yet the core processes are robust and roll on. I have experienced other organisations that appeared to be driven more by the personality of key individuals, with the underlying processes being weak and subject to radical change. This can lead to more short-term and 'knee jerk' decision-making, less underpinned by process and consistency. To me this has a variety of causes:

- Imbalance of control and influence in a management group that cannot deal effectively with conflict.

- The inability to say 'no' and *The Emperor's New Clothes* scenario where no one dares to point out the obvious.

- Unchecked enthusiasm in a business run more by personality than process.

- Immaturity in someone with authority who acts like the proverbial 'kid in a sweet shop' reaching out for everything, because they can.

- An element of greed—we can 'have a piece of that'—without a full evaluation of the opportunity.

- Ignorance of the true costs (time, money, resources) and implications.

Some of these elements combined can result in 'toxic positivity'. I have witnessed and been frustrated by this during my career. Whilst knee-jerk, ill-considered reactions to every problem, issue or challenge are neither required nor constructive (i.e. flapping and panic), toxic positivity can prove just as damaging to an organisation as apathy.

I've encountered senior people insistent on holding off confronting or communicating issues to an extent that it can border on dishonesty. They can demonstrate a steadfast refusal to accept the reality staring them in the face because of their overly optimistic belief that things may improve. Instead of a transparent, open approach when a problem arises, they keep covering it up, hoping it will get better. Eventually they have an even bigger, costlier mess to deal with.

I won't stray too far into areas where I don't really have the competence to add much value. Therefore, I would encourage readers to study David Snowden's Cynefin framework, which assesses the difference between complicated and complex systems.

Kellogg's Krispy Bisks—the launch that never was

Some of the previous points become manifest in the story of Kellogg's Krispy Bisks.

There were certain similarities between Kellogg's and Procter & Gamble, historic US multinationals with strong positions in their respective categories. Whilst Procter & Gamble typically 'lock horns' with Unilever in detergents, Kellogg's arch-rival in UK breakfast cereals was Weetabix.

Kellogg's were the overall cereal category leaders through their flaked (Cornflakes, Frosties, Special K) and rice-based products (Rice Krispies, Coco Pops). Weetabix were number two overall but dominated in biscuit-based and hot cereals. Cereal Partners Worldwide (Nestle/General Mills) were also consistently growing shares and private label products were grabbing a greater piece of the action.

A year or so before I joined, Kellogg's had appointed a blunt, straight-talking Australian as UK MD who had come in and started to shake up the business. One of his key acts was to make a new sales director appointment, promoting a bright, driven and ambitious internal candidate, who clearly had an eye for talent and recruited yours truly! One of their objectives was to go on the front foot against key competitors whilst simultaneously driving hard on Kellogg's core brands.

To take on Weetabix's dominance in breakfast biscuit cereals, Kellogg's marketing and innovation team set out to develop a top-class product to challenge them. Through consumer research, they identified that Weetabix's weakness to certain consumers was that the products turned soft and mushy quite quickly when milk was poured over. Great for feeding infants and toddlers, but less desirable for older consumers. A product was then developed that would retain its crispiness longer in milk and the brand name was agreed—Kellogg's Krispy Bisks.

This was a major, high profile initiative for Kellogg's UK and my responsibility was to lead the sales input within the project team. A significant amount of time and funding was invested as this was such a strategic play, including full use of BASES testing (a simulated test marketing tool suite). We were confident that we had a winner!

Artwork and branding were developed, and an advertising campaign was commissioned to emphasise the crispiness of the product in milk. Distribution targets with key customers were set and a full in-store promotion and point of sale material plan were developed. We then started to go and sell customers on this fantastic new launch for the cereal category and the results were encouraging with strong distribution agreements secured with the key grocery multiples.

What could go wrong?

Not a lot really; we were on the edge of glory except for one relatively minor detail…the manufacture of the product itself.

Kellogg's did not have the manufacturing capability to produce biscuit-like products and searching Europe for a manufacturer who could produce enough product for the launch did not prove fruitful. A year or so before, Kellogg's had launched an extruded cereal called Crispix that was produced in the Far East and shipped across. An extruded cereal is one where several different grains are all mashed together, extruded into the required shape, and then baked. Typically, they were quite strong products that held their form well. In Crispix's case, this was a lattice product.

A similar arrangement was proposed for Krispy Bisks when a manufacturer with sufficient capacity was identified in Australia. I remember sitting in the project meeting when this was proposed and like my other colleagues, nodding and deferring to our supply chain colleagues' greater knowledge. A few comments were made in private afterwards, but no one spoke up to challenge the wisdom of shipping container loads of light, brittle wheat biscuits halfway around the world. The emperor may well have been naked, but we cracked on with the launch plans.

Initial product samples for customers were air freighted over straight from the production line and all was good. We were on to a winner and the pipeline stocks were due to arrive a week or so before our go-live day in-store.

Then came an early morning call from the sales director to attend an urgent project update meeting.

The first stock had arrived and when the container had been opened and samples checked, the bisks had broken up and crumbled into a powder. Further quality control checks would be done, but we needed to be ready to advise customers.

Disaster! Pretty much every box opened was the same; the launch would have to be cancelled ten days or so before it hit the customers' shelves. Promotions had been booked, Krispy Bisks had been included on new shelf layout planograms and the sales teams had to make embarrassed, red-faced phone calls to customers and deal with the ensuing demands for compensation, and costs of re-doing planograms, etc.

However, if ever I experienced a case of the *Emperor's New Clothes* in my career, then this was it. With hindsight, it was a crazy logistical plan to ship a delicate product across the seven seas, but no one had the foresight or courage to offer persistent dissension to the plan (myself included). In a dark reference to the Russian Kursk submarine disaster that had taken place just before, it was observed that 'Kursky Bisks' were better off at the bottom of the sea.

False rumours later circulated that Weetabix had paid Kellogg's to stop the launch, which saved Kellogg's some face and in the highly unlikely event it was true, it was well above my pay grade. Sometimes, unexpected external events can also act to your advantage. Attention was quickly diverted away from Krispy Bisks as a UK fuel crisis commanded the highest priority focus for retailers and suppliers alike. Ensuring continuity of supply across the whole store enabled Krispy Bisks to slip into the shadows, with embarrassment minimised and forgotten by most. A year later, the Jo Moore affair brought the phrase 'a good day to bury bad news' to the public attention (see next chapter). The difference being, Kellogg's benefited by circumstance, not by calculation and cynicism.

(As a footnote, despite the Krispy Bisk disaster, interestingly, the UK MD eventually became CEO in the US.)

From my perspective, I was determined to be wary of *Emperor's New Clothes* syndrome going forward and decided that if ever I had fundamental concerns or even nagging doubts about a project, I would air them. This transpired quite quickly when I moved across into a marketing role on children's cereals. The consistent rise of Cheerios was proving a thorn in Kellogg's side as they did not have an extruded multi-grain product that could compete. We set to work to produce a product under the Rice Krispies banner, as a contemporary offering from Snap, Crackle & Pop (the three elves who promote the brand). Instead of one shape, to increase kids' interaction with the food, we produced a series of shapes like trees, people, stars, etc (similar to the old Heinz Noodle Doodle brand).

The product created seemed good enough, especially with the addition of prebiotics to aid the digestive system (this is why I spent a day discussing poo and wind as mentioned in Chapter 6) and Snap, Crackle & Pop were certainly up for it! The problem was deciding on a name. Various brand naming agencies were consulted over quite a length of time to get a perfect name. Cheerios has a nice, positive up-beat sound to it, so when the name finally proposed was presented, I just had to put my hand up to object. To me, Muddles was too negative sounding. My daughter was four at the time and a target audience for the product. As a parent I did not want my child getting in a muddle, it just wasn't a positive vibe. I offered Snapseez as an alternative, the idea being that kids could match up the shapes. Not a great name either, though I considered it to have less negativity than Muddles. I was over-ruled, and it launched as Muddles. Not that long afterwards when I'd moved to AG Barr, I noticed in a store that the product name had changed to Kellogg's Rice Krispies Multi Grain Shapes—wow! What a slick name, it just rolls off a toddler's tongue!!

A few points to ponder

- **Be a student of simplicity and not an arch overcomplicator.**

- **Think of simple, Scalextric type solutions and avoid the complications of Hornby.**

- **If you spot something that others can't (or don't want to) see, ask: is the emperor really wearing new clothes?**

CHAPTER 15

SEEING THROUGH THE MIST

What can be done to aid prioritisation, help people see through the mist and understand what is most important?

As AG Barr's portfolio started to expand through NPD and product acquisitions, the sales team became confused as to which brands and initiatives were most important and how much of their time and focus should go towards different projects. To help them, I went back to another old, but familiar model—Maslow's Hierarchy of Needs, where lower order needs must be met before you can move up to the next levels of the pyramid. I compared this to our product portfolio.

In most FMCG businesses there tend to be a few core brands or products that effectively underpin everything else. They contribute the most sales and profit, but also generate production efficiencies and economies of scale benefitting newer, smaller, or more specialised brands. Sometimes this can be captured by the 80/20 or Pareto concept, that is, twenty per cent of the product range produces eighty per cent of the sales. Keeping these products in good health and performing well are the 'Basic Needs' of the organisation. Failure to manage this carefully in the here and now will undermine attempts to grow the business by launching new products and ideas, which rely on profit generated by the established brands for investment.

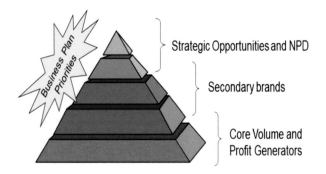

In AG Barr, the Basic Need brand which was the core volume and profit generator by far was IRN-BRU. Barr had traditionally positioned itself as the IRN-BRU company, though over time we focused on becoming Barr Soft Drinks, representing a change in philosophy, not just name. At Kellogg's, standard cornflakes were key. Not only were Kellogg's Cornflakes a category and grocery icon, but they were the base for two other crucial products. With added sugar they became Frosties and with the addition of nuts and honey they were Crunchy Nut Cornflakes. Reflecting this, Kellogg's manufacturing facility at Trafford Park, Manchester where they were made, was the biggest cereal factory in the world.

At Flavour Warehouse where I briefly worked, even if you took out most of their e-liquid flavours, they would still have a very viable business from just two: Pinkman and Heisenberg.

Applying the Maslow analogy to the AG Barr product portfolio identified to the sales team which brands represented their 'bread and butter'. Of course, they were not permitted to ignore other products and were also measured on NPD results, but it ensured they had clear priorities.

The other common analogy with which most are familiar is of course the good old 'leaky bucket', where it is no good investing in NPD and initiatives to pour new business in at the top if your base business dribbles away through holes in the bottom of the bucket.

Ponder the following

- **In business, it is unwise to concentrate too much on the pennies, because the pounds will not take care of themselves!**

NB: Maslow's Hierarchy of Needs is clearly showing its age. Had it been developed today it would probably be more like this:

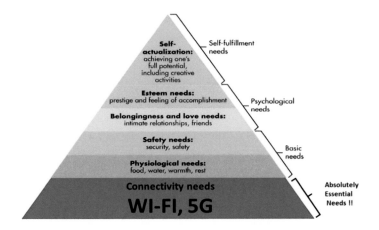

CHAPTER 16

FUN AND GAMES

Promotion is one of the classical four Ps of marketing (along with product, price and place) that I was taught at university. Promotion in its broadest sense refers to all activities designed to create awareness and encourage purchase of a brand, product or service. This includes TV and print advertising, public relations and these days of course, online presence and social media.

In FMCG it is the brand managers who typically have responsibility for all the activities run from the product packaging itself (competitions, mail-ins, etc), within the packaging (for example, a free toy in a cereal pack), or through vehicles such as TV, websites, radio or print. With the brand characters Kellogg's created, such as Tony the Tiger, Coco-Monkey, Snap, Crackle & Pop and Captain Ric (Ricicles), and with the high-profile sponsorships they secured, such as Disney, Warner Brothers, Star Wars and British Athletics (to name but a few), there was always great fun to be had.

Similarly, at AG Barr, IRN-BRU linked up with the Scottish and English Football Leagues and Super League Rugby. Rubicon was the official soft drink of the England and Wales cricket team, and Rockstar had some really exciting tie ups with professional boxing matches (Hatton versus Mayweather, Froch versus Groves), mixed martial arts, computer game releases and various music festivals.

In an FMCG sales role, the promotions on which most time and effort is spent are the ones shoppers see when they enter a store. These are executed by the retailers. Most in-store promotional offers these days tend to be simple price reductions or multi-buy offers, for example, 'buy three for five pounds'. Many graduates starting an FMCG career will have been given a promotional effectiveness project at some point. When I arrived at Kellogg's in 1999, they had invested in a software package called Trade Promotion Management (TPM) to provide such analysis. However, it worked by analysing past promotions and the promotional landscape had changed dramatically with the emergence of everyday low pricing (EDLP) instead of promotions and Safeway's extremely deep price cut promotions (pricing guerrilla tactics called Gonzalez). All the sales controllers knew that TPM was of little use by that point, but as the newcomer I was given the 'hospital pass' and had to tell the European president that a project he had championed and provided significant investment for was already obsolete.

Occasionally, you do see something quite different, but typically neither retailers nor suppliers have the patience for or want the complication of running more elaborate activities. That wasn't always the case and I've been involved with various brands and customers where, in conjunction with buying a certain product, the shopper would be rewarded with a free gift with their purchase, such as breakfast bowls, drinking glasses, towels, storage vessels, etc.

Persistence Pays

When I joined Kellogg's there were recurring discussions in business planning sessions about how it would be great to have a Kellogg-branded free cereal bowl promotion in the key grocery stores, but it was considered a sort of 'Holy Grail' promotion that would never be achieved. It was a challenge I took on and eventually we did indeed run several such promotions that performed really well. First, we utilised Kellogg's sponsorship of British Athletics to execute a free Olympic bowl in 2000. Only a couple of customers agreed to execute it due to the complexity, yet it performed well as customers could take home a free, high-quality ceramic bowl when they purchased two packs of Kellogg's cereal. We ran a similar promotion the following year, though just on Crunchy Nut Cornflakes and with more customers participating, the promotion gained momentum.

The FIFA Football World Cup in 2002 was taking place in Japan and South Korea. Unusually, this meant that matches in the UK would kick off in the morning due to the time difference. Large sporting events are crucial sales opportunities for brands and retailers, though in this case, (apart from diehards) the opportunity for beers, wines and spirits was appreciably less. This *was* an opportunity for breakfast products, though, until David Beckham fired in a late free-kick against Greece, England's participation was in the balance. With Wembley being rebuilt, the game was played at Manchester United's ground at Old Trafford— just a few hundred yards from Kellogg's head office. Fate.

After three years of patience and persistence trying to convince all the major UK retailers to manage the complexity of a free bowl promotion, we had our chance. By this point, I was leading Kellogg's Tesco and Sainsbury's sales teams and through lots of hard work and negotiation, we led the way. For every two packets of certain Kellogg's cereals, the consumer got a free ceramic breakfast bowl, designed on the outside like a traditional panel football and with the colour green inside with football pitch markings. We had advertising support on TV and posters. Eventually, 1.2 million bowls ended up in UK homes. We also received a global Kellogg Award for the year's best promotion.

The crowning glory was planned to be TV coverage of a World Cup sportsman's dinner that Kellogg's had agreed to sponsor for Caravan, the grocery industry charity. The event was at Preston North End's football stadium and all the surviving members of England's 1966 World Cup team (excluding Sir Bobby Charlton) were due to attend. TV and press coverage were lined up by our public relations team and Tony the Tiger was looking forward to meeting the World Cup heroes.

Unfortunately, footballer Roy Keane then intervened! He had walked out of the Republic of Ireland training camp at the World Cup and all the press wanted to do was interview Jack Charlton, the former Ireland manager. My poor bowls! They missed out on their moment of glory, though I did enjoy the company of a footballing hero, the late Alan Ball, until the early hours of the morning.

The Man in the Hathaway Shirt

There was a famous printed advertisement in the 1950s for Hathaway shirts created by David Ogilvy. Many marketeers will be familiar with the iconic image of the distinguished man with an eyepatch promoting and ultimately transforming the sales of the Hathaway shirt company in Maine. The eyepatch was never mentioned in the advert but used as a mysterious prop to generate curiosity.

On a creative marketing course that I attended with Kellogg's, we studied this landmark piece of advertising, or rather, we studied a video of others analysing it. Of course, the main discussion was around the eyepatch—what did it add? Was it distasteful and should it be removed? Whilst there was no real relevance to the eyepatch and several in the group said it should be removed, various compromises were assessed. The conclusion was that removing it diluted a very powerful advert into a relatively bland piece of copy, which wouldn't stand out.

Flexibility can be a very important quality in business, but the man in the Hathaway shirt proves that sometimes *compromise* can be a dirty word and ultimately render an idea worthless. I hold up my hand to making some compromises during my career, with possibly the most pointless one being a promotion as an account manager working at Asda.

It was the run-up to Christmas and both the Pampers (nappies) brand manager and the Always (sanitary towels) brand managers were insistent on having in-store promotions. 'All the promotion slots and display spaces are booked up,' I replied. 'The only way you can get a promotion is if you provide a separate stand-alone display shipper unit and they have to be Christmas-branded.' The brand managers insisted it was crucial, and I felt compelled to find a compromise. We sent flat-packed cardboard Father Christmas display shippers incorporating the message 'Buy Pampers, Get Always Half Price' to stores so that they could load them with stock and site them in the health and beauty aisle. The brand managers were pleased—in theory, they had their promotions. In practice, it was a desperate waste of time and money. If even a dozen shippers got to the shop floor I would have been surprised and there was a problem scanning the promotion in-store for the first few days. I learned that if you compromise too much you might as well not bother.

On another occasion at Procter & Gamble, a brand manager brought a 'fantastic idea' to me called the 'Lenortainer'. At the time, fabric conditioners were in plastic bottles as they still are, but Procter & Gamble had also introduced cardboard refill packs to reduce plastic waste. The Lenortainer was a de-luxe Lenor bottle to be sold for ninety-nine pence and sited next to the refills. 'It has to be empty,' said the brand manager, 'as we can't fill this bottle on the production line.' I was slightly taken aback. 'So, you want me to go Tesco, Morrisons and Asda and ask them to sell bottles of fresh air?' Needless to say, the Lenortainer never happened!

A Salutary Lesson

At Kellogg's, many people developed a fascination or even an obsession with Tony the Tiger and Frosties. Tony had been trying hard on Frosties' behalf for many years, but unfortunately, sales weren't 'grrreat'. In fact, whilst still one of the largest brands by volume in the portfolio, sales had been declining year after year. Every senior manager or marketeer seemed determined to be the person who fixed Frosties, so it became a bit of a political football. So much so that the CEO in Battle Creek got involved with the production of UK TV advertising at one point, due to escalating viewpoints in the Kellogg's and J Walter Thompson hierarchies. (JWT was the advertising agency. Along with Kellogg's brand managers, marketing managers, marketing director and so on, JWT personnel wanted to be recognised as the ones who fixed this iconic, much loved but troubled brand.)

The TV copy at the time had introduced a new villain, the evil Dr Cheetah, as Tony's arch-rival who was determined to steal the Frosties secret formula. Dr Cheetah sported a menacing eyepatch, though he did not wear a Hathaway shirt! Entertaining as the 'Batmanesque' advert was, it wasn't having a tangibly positive effect, so in the brand planning sessions we decided that a more dramatic intervention was required.

A couple of years previously, before I had joined, a move towards brand efficiencies had seen the Coco Pops brand re-named Choco Krispies, consistent with continental Europe. However, there were quite a few disgruntled customers at the time (an era in which P&G changed Oil of Ulay to Oil of Olay and Jif became Cif for similar reasons). The Coco Pops advertising agency, Leo Burnett's, hit on a radical idea which was one of the first truly interactive campaigns: The Coco Vote. Kellogg's decided to let UK consumers decide on the brand name. TV adverts were run with campaigners championing the names Coco Pops and Choco Krispies while consumers were encouraged to vote via a freephone number, or online (though it was still early days for the internet in the late nineties).

The result? An absolute landslide victory for Coco Pops. TV copy celebrated the result, the packaging was changed back and Leo Burnett in my mind had pulled off a game-changing piece of advertising.

Returning to Frosties, as a sales and marketing team we discussed various ideas to re-invigorate Tony and the brand. One of the more radical questions asked was 'has Tony had his day?'. Was the aging Tiger too long in the tooth and no longer relevant as we started the twenty-first century? To remove Tony from the packaging and change the advertising strategy would be a major departure and even though his appeal may have faded with consumers, he was a very much-loved feline within the Kellogg's company.

Thinking back to the Coco Vote, I pondered if we could engage consumers once more and see if we could ride a wave of affection for Tony if we threatened to dispense with his services. We then developed a cunning plan that Dr Cheetah would kidnap Tony and hold him to ransom. The public would have to pay a million-lid ransom to get him back. Tony's image on the Frosties box would be removed and left as a blank shadow, whilst a pre-paid postcard would be printed on the box that kids could send in to help free Tony (with an online execution too, as this was 2001!). We would provide TV updates and when a million lids had been received (or fewer if we considered it appropriate—this was a marketing plan, not a general election!) we would celebrate Tony's release, he would regain the public's affection and reclaim pride of place on the packaging. We all, myself especially, thought this would be a magnificent, highly visible campaign that would restore Tony and Frosties' pre-eminence in kids' cereal...

But...

After all our hard work and enthusiasm, the UK board refused to sign off the campaign. I was absolutely gutted. Like everyone else, I wanted to be the person who fixed Frosties. I wanted that honour and recognition, yet a brilliant plan was turned down. My initial anger subsided to feelings of disappointment as the board explained that if there was an incident of a high-profile kidnapping or similar unfortunate event whilst the campaign was running, it would be in appalling bad taste to society, hugely detrimental to the brand image and cost a fortune if we had to remove the product from stores in a damage limitation exercise. I was frustrated but overruled.

Several months later, on a sunny afternoon in Kellogg's Manchester headquarters, after we had cobbled together an alternative though much weaker Frosties campaign, a colleague popped into my office and said, 'Have you heard the news? Someone has flown a plane into the Twin Towers in New York!' Everyone gathered around a small TV set and watched the awful footage. On 11th September 2001, four airliners had been hijacked, effectively kidnapping hundreds of people in the worst terrorist atrocity in history. It was a moment that those who witnessed can never forget.

External events had helped the failure of the Krispy Bisks launch disappear from view a year earlier. However, Jo Moore, a government advisor, gained instant notoriety and was forced to make a public apology when a leaked memo revealed she'd suggested that the September 11th attacks were a 'good day to bury bad news'. Now that was just callous!

Had the Frosties Million Lid Ransom campaign been running at the time this would have been hugely distasteful and highly damaging for Kellogg's corporate reputation. The board had been right to block the Frosties' campaign. I was wrong and learned several lessons that day. Most notably, that no matter how good a business idea you think you have, you need to retain a degree of objectivity and be open to the counsel of others. Persistence and tenacity can be important qualities in business, but a sense of perspective is also vital.

As an aside, when I joined AG Barr in 2004, they had just launched a new TV campaign on IRN-BRU. The advertising idea was that the taste of IRN-BRU was so phenomenal that the person drinking it became so engrossed that they would miss unbelievable and incredible events unfolding around them. One of the TV adverts showed a homeless person swept up and processed through a street sweeper vehicle and emerging clean, well dressed and all 'spic and span'. Glasgow is IRN-BRU's heartland and ten years later a tragedy occurred on the 22nd of December 2014 when a bin lorry collided with pedestrians in the city centre, killing six and injuring fifteen others. Timing can be crucial and clearly that advert is unlikely to ever be shown again.

A Snap and Crackle of An Idea That Went Pop!

When I moved on to brand managing a portfolio of Kellogg's kids' brands in my penultimate assignment in Old Trafford, my daughter was just a toddler herself. Like most children, she loved having stories read to her at bedtime, but such was her appetite that we often let someone else do the narration using story-time compact discs (CDs).

We had a gap in the on-pack promotional plan for Rice Krispies and needed a brand-building idea that could develop the character of the elves Snap, Crackle and Pop and drive sales. Inspired by my daughter, I came up with the idea of a series of story-time CDs that would be free in the pack. Snap, Crackle and Pop had distinct personalities with Snap being the eldest, cleverest and most serious, Crackle the strong, silent type who provided the muscle, and Pop being the youngest, silliest elf who was invariably a source of amusement to the others. Snap, Crackle and Pop would host the CD, like a kind of elven Ant and Dec. As well as their banter and songs, each CD would feature several fairy stories. As most fairy stories contain an important message, Snap would help the other two (and the listening children) understand the moral of the tale. For example, *The Ugly Duckling* would encourage children not to judge others by how they looked and *The Boy Who Cried Wolf* would reinforce the danger of telling lies.

We commissioned an agency to work up scripts and songs for three different CDs and though it was a costly promotion I was convinced we were onto a winner. I had a vision of millions of kids bonding with Snap,

Crackle and Pop and learning important life lessons on car journeys or while tucked up in bed at night.

Whilst the Million Lid Ransom understandably and rightly never came to fruition, it is one of my key regrets that the Rice Krispies' story-time CDs project had to be suddenly stopped and never reached the public. Kellogg's secured a new high-profile licence which took precedence to feature on all the key brands at the time the CDs were planned. Several years later I noticed McDonald's giving story CDs as the gift with a Happy Meal and sighed as I knew that Snap, Crackle and Pop would have done a far better job!

A few points to ponder

- **Persistence and resilience are often key when you are trying to do something different.**

- **However, if an idea becomes diluted and compromised you may be best advised to drop it and move on to something else.**

- **Don't allow yourself to become too involved or attached to a project. Retaining an element of objectivity is key.**

- **Decisions in business are rarely personal.**

'Many, many thanks from all at Booker for the contribution you have made to our business with AG Barr. You will be a big loss though we look forward to working with you in the future and if we can help, just shout. All the very best, Charles and all your friends at Booker.'

Charles Wilson, CEO of Booker Wholesale.

'Thank you for all your help. We've had a strong relationship with AG Barr and whilst we have not always seen eye-to-eye or gained agreement, the business has moved forward considerably and always outstripped growth of many larger suppliers with considerably more resources available. You were never afraid of tension and always had customers and the Barr business at the heart of everything you did. Talent, skill and experience always count.'

David Beardmore, UK Grocery Director, Tesco.

'Your leaving is a real shame to hear as you were doing a great job working with us.'

Dawood Pervez, Managing Director of Bestway Wholesale.

'You've always been a voice of reason and you're one of the good guys in the industry who knows it inside out.'

John C Baines, Trading Director Unitas Wholesale.

A SENSE OF PERSPECTIVE

On one of the training courses when I started with Procter & Gamble, one of the senior managers who recognised that we were all young, determined, career-focused individuals wanted to provide a sense of perspective. He espoused the idea 'of course business and your job are really important' but with oblique reference to Maslow he also commented on the need for 'a sense of perspective—after all, you're only selling soap powder and there are people in this country living on the streets in cardboard boxes'. I rather frivolously responded, 'Yes, but the more we sell, the more boxes they have to sleep in!' The comment achieved a round of laughter and got me onto the manager's radar but was not the most sensitive comment I have ever made.

Thirty or so years later, with more maturity and greater humility, I observed the changes in society brought on by the Covid-19 crisis, the subsequent lockdown and social distancing measures. These certainly caused most people to think differently about our key workers and the role they perform in society. Nurses, medical staff and carers were at the forefront of efforts to keep us safe, with the police, military and various other public sector employers keeping the country running while the rest of us grumbled about the restrictions and worried about whether we would be able to go back to our jobs and careers.

The public outpouring of support, particularly for the NHS, helped to uplift the nation but the key concern is whether the 'NHS Heroes' will still be remembered as prominently in the future. It has been recognised by many that nurses, in particular, are not sufficiently financially rewarded for the care they provide, and most public sector workers do not earn as much as their counterparts in private sector careers. There are so many other key workers who should be rewarded.

I was totally humbled by the story below on LinkedIn and compelled to comment, 'We are all in debt to the NHS. "Hats off" to their courage and commitment. Very humbling for those of us spending careers in business, just chasing the £££s.'

'Short story from a young NHS Nurse.

This is how I left work this morning, after sobbing during staff handover. I feel it reflects the sad reality of how NHS staff are feeling every day at the moment.

Tonight, on my shift I had to tell the family of a dying man, that they cannot go in to see him, they cannot say goodbye to their dad and that they have to go home.

Think about that for a minute, how it must feel to tell a family that.

This is after finding out one of my patients had died yesterday after testing positive for the corona virus. I know this is happening all over but the patient group I look after, I really feel they don't deserve this. Battling cancer with every fibre of their being, having chemo, radiotherapy and everything that comes with that and then to die alone, unable to have visitors, say goodbye to their loved ones. Wards unable to support their family the way we want to because family can't visit. How can this be happening, how is this fair? How on earth will families get closure? Can you imagine your parent dying along and not being allowed to see them?

Don't the public want to do their bit to stop this from happening? Why is it so hard to just stay inside? And the truth is I'm filled with dread, because I know this is going to get worse.'

Similarly, shop workers kept us supplied with key provisions whilst being at much higher risk of contracting the virus through daily interaction with the general public. They too tend to be at the bottom end of retailers' salary scales.

A friend, the Liverpudlian comedian, author and historian John Martin made many supportive and humorous posts during the lockdown, recognising the bravery of others, encouraging all to play their part and lifting spirits through comedy.

There are three courageous and inspirational people from my hometown who have continually helped me to keep a perspective on life, though their stories are very different.

Steve Prescott MBE

The late Steve Prescott made a massive contribution to one of my most enjoyable days out when his two tries in the Wembley sunshine helped St Helens beat Bradford Bulls in a classic Rugby League Challenge Cup final in 1996. However, that was just the start of a courageous and inspirational story.

Ten years on and Steve was diagnosed with pseudomyxoma peritonei, a rare and terminal form of cancer. He was determined to win his fight with cancer and succeeded when he underwent a pioneering multi-visceral transplant in 2013. Tragically, he succumbed to post-operative complications.

After the shock of his initial diagnosis, Steve set up the Steve Prescott Foundation and embarked on a series of incredible endurance events to raise money for Christies Cancer Hospital in Manchester and the RFL Benevolent Fund. Steve's initiative and leadership united the sport of Rugby League with players past and present supporting gruelling challenges including marathons, the Three Peaks, Land's End to John o' Groats and events in the local community—all whilst under treatment for an incredibly debilitating disease. 'The body achieves what the mind believes,' became his mantra and what he achieved physically was unbelievable.

Steve's courage and strength were there for all to see. On the inside, his drive was to show people that the cancer would not stop him from living life to the full and to inspire others to overcome their adversity and meet challenges head-on. He certainly had a major impact on me, and I cherish having a small part in his story by participating in some of the events and securing AG Barr's support.

Steve's wife Linzi completed his biography the year after he passed and, whilst he never showed it, to read about the physical agony he had to endure leaves me shaken yet bursting with admiration for how he coped. Steve and his family remain a hugely positive influence in St Helens and the Rugby League community. The Player of the Year in Super League is now aptly called The Steve Prescott Man of Steel Award. His foundation continues a tradition of community events and fund-raising challenges supporting the charities and a research fund to study pseudomyxoma peritonei and related conditions. Steve Prescott was one in a million.

Andy Reid MBE

In 2009, Andy lost both of his legs and an arm serving his country in Afghanistan. After being flown back to the UK, Andy astounded people with his recovery by spending only two weeks in hospital being treated for his injuries before he was ready to make his first trip home. Since then, he has become a successful local businessman and inspired others as a passionate ambassador for the Soldiers' Charity and other amputees, helping raise funds and awareness. He has performed skydives, taken part in the Steve Prescott Foundation St Helen's 10K Run, abseiled down the Big One in Blackpool and performed countless other activities.

Andy is also an accomplished motivational speaker. His autobiography, *Standing Tall: The Inspirational Story of a True British Hero,* was published in 2013 and is a powerful read.

When I was a kid in the seventies, my favourite comic book was called *Warlord*. It glamorised the Second World War and featured a series of ridiculous characters 'socking it to Jerry' and 'kicking Japanese butts'. After you have visited the war cemeteries at Ypres and Normandy and met a true hero like Andy Reid and seen him running a 10K on two prosthetic legs, it is embarrassing to have been entertained by such dross.

Damian Harper

Damian and I met when we started high school in 1980 and have been close friends ever since. He is a person of immense courage who I have held in utmost admiration for over forty years.

When we were seventeen, Damian developed bone cancer in his left knee and had to have his whole leg amputated. On top of that, he required intensive chemotherapy and I can never forget visiting him in hospital and remembering how ill he was. As soon as he was able, he got back on with his life. Instead of returning to his A-levels he went to work for the NHS, passed his driving test and refused to let the loss of his leg prevent him from doing what most teenage boys want to do. He came out to the pub every week, chatted to girls, got drunk with the rest of us, hit the dance floor and still moved better than most. One evening, a group of us went out for a drink and at last orders he was reluctant to go home. 'I have some test results coming back tomorrow,' he said, 'and basically I'll find out if I'm going to live or die.'

Thankfully Damian's test results were okay and over time he was able to do most of the things we all enjoyed—watching football, rugby and having crazy nights out and weekends away. He progressed at work, studied for a degree, and bought a house with his partner Sue.

Unfortunately, there was little to no support or counselling for Damian in those days and bravely getting on with life suppressed post-traumatic stress disorder, which surfaced in his forties with severe mental and emotional challenges. Life had cruelly knocked him again but with the support of Sue and digging deep into his reserves of determination he battled demons and inspired others.

As a trustee of the Amputation Foundation, he now supports others affected like him and was part of an amputee group who climbed Kilimanjaro. He has made several TV appearances and featured in a BBC Four documentary, *No Body's Perfect*, culminating in a picture of Damian radiating power and confidence, taken by renowned photographer Rankin. He is also developing a career as a male model, with London Fashion week now a fixture in his diary.

Damian is a brave and incredible human being and I'm very proud to be his friend.

We can all understandably become anxious or stressed about jobs and careers. However, before they can even consider their work aspirations, Damian and Andy have massive physical, mental, and emotional challenges to overcome that most of us cannot even begin to imagine.

It is unequivocally humbling to know people like Steve Prescott, Andy Reid, and Damian Harper. I hoped that if I ever had a serious setback like they've endured, I would be able to find a fraction of their courage.

No way, that couldn't have happened to him, could it?

I didn't plan to include this story initially. It just didn't feel right, as despite having a serious setback, unlike Andy and Damian I have been able to continue my career without major limitations. However, after meeting Nick Clarke from the charity Stroke Information, I'm hoping that sharing this experience may give hope and encouragement to others.

During 2015, and probably before that if I think back, I had what I described as a few 'funny turns' where I'd say sentences the wrong way round or mumble my words. I was prone to feeling a bit light-headed and having the odd headache at times which I'd just dismissed as fatigue or not having enough coffee. With a busy schedule, a responsible job and lots of travel, I didn't think much about it and just cracked on with things.

That summer at AG Barr had been hectic after the implementation of a huge operating systems project.

Our family holiday was a well-earned break in Cornwall and one day as I sat on a deck chair relaxing, I tried to say something, but no words came out. I nodded off and thought it was just another funny turn. When we got home the following week, I went to the gym for a spin class, came home and made lunch.

I then went to my daughter's room to ask her to tidy up her holiday gear and when I went to speak, pure 'gobbledegook' came out for about 10 mins. I knew what I wanted to say but it just made odd sounds. We both ended up laughing at my predicament and I resorted to sign language to tell my daughter what I needed her to do.

I then had a strange feeling as if my head was floating all afternoon. I thought, 'this isn't right' and booked in with my GP the next morning. I have a fabulous GP and she identified straight away that I may have had a transient ischaemic attack (TIA or mini-stroke). She asked my wife to take me straight to hospital.

I had various scans and tests and it was bizarre to be pushed to a stroke ward in a wheelchair even though I could walk and function normally. After all the scans, a left lobal infarct was diagnosed. I'd not heard of an infarct before, but it means a small, localised area of dead tissue resulting from a blood supply failure. As often happens with TIAs a full ischaemic stroke had followed.

It all seemed quite surreal and like it wasn't happening. I was forty-six years old and 'fit as a fiddle'—how could this happen to me? There appeared to be no obvious reason for the stroke, though later tests revealed I had a significant hole in my heart. This isn't uncommon and many people go through their life totally oblivious of having one. However, if a blood clot gets through the hole you are in trouble.

When we got home, I was exhausted. I got into bed thinking about what had happened and suddenly began sobbing uncontrollably. My mum had died suddenly of a brain haemorrhage when she was forty-seven and her mother had had multiple strokes in her old age. I think if anything, the tears were ones of relief that I was still here.

Fortunately, I was left with no real physical issues. My sense of balance isn't quite as good. I frequently bang into door frames but that's about it. I had the hole in my heart plugged with a PFO closure operation at Liverpool Heart and Chest Hospital in April 2016. It's a fascinating procedure that was performed under local anaesthetic so I could watch. I ran a marathon a year later with a better time than my first one. With a little titanium plug in my heart, I can joke that I'm now one per cent of being a terminator—one of my favourite series of films.

I probably went back to work too quickly. AG Barr was supportive, but I didn't want to fall behind or lose my self-confidence. I pushed myself to perform exactly as I had previously done and when you do that people tend to forget what you've been through.

The stroke's impact on me is hidden. It has resulted in fatigue, delayed memory recall and depression. These can be difficult to manage but they're nothing like the physical and mental challenges that Andy and Damian have to overcome. I count myself very lucky as it could have been so much worse. I look at the BBC journalist Andrew Marr, who has had a much tougher battle from a similar incident.

Strokes do not just affect older people and can have a devastating effect. If you ever experience loss of speech or have 'funny turns', don't ignore them; get checked out. There are thousands of worthy charities people can support, but please be aware of the terrible trauma that affects stroke survivors and the people close to them.

REFLECTION

Catalysts

Culture eats strategy for breakfast – Peter Drucker.

When I joined Procter and Gamble in 1990, I assumed I would work there until I retired. It was a marvellous blue-chip company with a real focus on developing its people. Richard Dupree, the post-war CEO, famously declared, 'If you leave us our money, our buildings and our brands, but take away our people, the Company will fail. But if you take away our money, our buildings and our brands, but leave us our people, we can rebuild the whole thing in a decade.' The formative years of my career were very much in a business that reflected Drucker's views.

In a way, I left Kellogg's because although it had many similarities with Procter & Gamble, it just wasn't the same, particularly in the areas of leadership and commitment to its people.

At AG Barr, for the first ten years or so, I had the autonomy to use my experience and principles to build the type of team environment that I had aspired to. We delivered fantastic results and comments from colleagues confirmed how much they enjoyed the environment.

Towards the end of my time at Barr, I knew that as an individual I was becoming somewhat stale and the company's results and culture were changing. From my perspective, we were heading in the opposite direction to Drucker's quote so when a conversation began about a restructure including my departure, it was unexpected, but ultimately quite welcomed.

After leaving AG Barr in the summer of 2019, I accepted a position as the chief commercial officer at Flavour Warehouse, a business specialising in smoking cessation (e-liquids and vaping), not a category I was ever going to become a consumer of. As a passionate anti-smoker, I considered vaping a much less harmful alternative for the vaper and particularly for third-party bystanders.

It was a fascinating change to be part of a successful, ambitious SME business and there was a lot about the role I enjoyed. There were multiple challenges across my remit of sales and marketing and some gaps in personnel to fit the structure I had proposed. A few things troubled me, like a lack of trust and transparency across the organisation, but I remained philosophical and considered that change in such areas would need to be influenced gradually.

I was quite shocked when my time at Flavour Warehouse was cut short. I had worked really hard and was making a positive impact but my services were suddenly no longer required without being given any real explanation.

Maybe I had been working for Uncle Joe? Certainly, there was minimal conviction for Drucker's beliefs. The net result was a need for some alchemy to turn my situation around. After a brief period of reflection, then the enforced inactivity of the first lockdown, the recipe for *Baked Alaska* began to form. I had thought about it for years, so it was now or never!

Self-Reflection

Someone reading this may think, 'Okay wise-guy, it's all very well to highlight the mistakes of others, but are you really qualified to comment? Many of your peers, others you worked with and some who worked for you, are now MDs and CEOs of some significant businesses, why aren't you one?'

That would be a fair question. I have thought about this a lot and I believe the answers come down to three factors: Style (KSA), Circumstances and Comparison.

Style

With good A-levels and an upper second degree in Business Studies, the intelligence is there. What I have lacked in the **knowledge** area has probably been due to switching off from work related subjects. I found 'talking shop' quite boring and tend to socialise less with work colleagues. When younger I worried about being judged if I had a few too many drinks and showed drunken antics as I would with my close friends.

I have never been one for leaving a training course and getting stuck into all the follow-up reading. Some articles and commentaries have had a tangible impact on me over the years, and I have usually participated wholeheartedly in training programs on the day. However, as an example, whilst GAP Partnership's training on negotiation is excellent, I have never been motivated enough to plough through every page of their accompanying book, *The 48 Laws of Power*.

I am very grateful for the support from my employers in developing my **skills.** As individuals, we all map out differently and I'd point to a strong track record in developing people and successful, productive relationships with customers. In the corporate world I have been less enthusiastic about the internal and analytical projects that tend to get you noticed by the highest-ranking officers. I have also been outspoken, having witnessed the damage caused by the Emperor's New Clothes. This is possibly the key reason that many of my peers have gone on to secure bigger and more influential roles. I commend and congratulate them as I haven't had the right blend to progress as far.

The final consideration is **attitude**—desire, behaviours, and hunger for success. I've had a successful career; however, I've sometimes lacked self-confidence, been resistant to change and probably been dogged by self-doubt and impostor syndrome. When I don't really know something or lack expertise in an area, it shows. I have seen others who carry this challenge with far greater aplomb. I was told early in my career that I was too open and honest ('wears his heart on his sleeve') and hence unlikely to make it beyond sales director—words that proved quite prophetic.

The legendary Dundee United Football Club manager Jim McClean used to stand on the touchline at training, screaming with frustration at the young, well-paid players coming through. He would bellow that 'they didn't want it' as much as he did. Maybe I haven't wanted it enough in the corporate world.

Circumstances

As described earlier, after starting in a great company where I could learn and develop, I probably ended up in the wrong environments for me to thrive, where there was less emphasis on leadership and culture and more focus on projects and analysis.

Maybe my style and qualities have just not been fully appreciated in environments where my skill set became less valued. However, As Bob Dylan once sang, 'the times they are a changin'' and the likes of Patrick Lencioni and Simon Sinek herald a new era where success is based on trust, transparency, vulnerability and appreciation of others. The way I have always operated and encouraged.

Whilst the Gospel of Matthew may have been written over two thousand years ago, it seems that now in business the 'salt of the earth' types are becoming much more appreciated and can lead organisations to great success.

Comparison

An interesting article in *GQ Magazine* by Jacqueline Hurst caught my eye in which she describes 'comparison as the thief of joy', going on to say that comparison is a waste of your time. Many of us commence our careers with specific aspirations, but over time I believe Maslow's model still holds true and once lower order needs have been met, esteem needs and self-actualisation needs differ massively as we are all unique. As Jacqueline says, 'Someone else's intelligence / body / financial status does not mean they are better than you.' The messages of gratitude and goodwill I received on leaving AG Barr meant far more to me than if I'd been given a better bonus that year. They are comments I will cherish for a long time and provide reassurance that in the most part I have done right by others. And that is coming from someone who, as a shallow twenty-one-year-old, splashed his graduation loan on a second-hand Rolex!

Comparison can be constructive if it's used as a benchmark to help you improve. Certainly, measuring your knowledge and skills against successful, more experienced operators can help significantly, though we've covered the danger of mimicking others' attitudes and behaviours and trying to be someone you're not.

Real Life Benchmark

Whilst searching through files and memorabilia for writing this book, I came across a card that a friend sent to me when my mother died unexpectedly during my second year at university. It was a very kind and considerate action that brought great comfort at the time. We had lived near to each other but had attended different schools, though we both studied for A-levels at the same sixth form college and rode the bus together every day. We eventually lost touch and I never knew until a few years ago that we had both followed careers in the grocery industry, myself on the supply side and Joanne in accountancy, before entering retail.

The Joanne referred to is Jo Whitfield, the CEO of Co-operative Food. I am delighted with Jo's success. To become the first female CEO of one of the big UK food retailers is a landmark achievement. Jo's kindness, consideration and decency are combined with an acute business brain. She is leading Co-operative to outstanding results and playing a vital role in our communities, particularly during the Covid-19 crisis. Jo is a fantastic example of a phenomenal business leader who has made it all the way and is most definitely 'salt of the earth'. She grew up a few houses away from Steve Prescott— such inspiration from one small street in St Helens!

A Source of Pride

The comedian Johnny Vegas and singer Jacqui Abbott of the Beautiful South are also from nearby. Our neighbours in Liverpool have long had a reputation for producing entertainers and they are never shy in letting the world know about it. St Helens is a much, much smaller town but is also a great source of talent on several fronts in the arts, sport and business.

Our town's original crest bears the Latin inscription *ex terra lucem* or 'light out of the earth'. As the post Covid-19 society continues to change around us, hopefully more and more people will realise that recognising and championing salt of the earth qualities can elevate us all to a higher plane.

MY NEW MISSION: BACK TO THE FUTURE

My new mission is going back to the future as a Business Doctor in my local area, to support and share my experience with businesses. I want to help them grow, achieve their vision and develop the wider economy in north west England.

A huge amount was invested in my training and development by the companies I've worked for and I enjoy passing on the learning from these powerful and transformational programmes, that may otherwise be beyond the resources of a typical SME. I am also sharing my experience by facilitating training through St Helens Chamber and have received the appropriate accreditation to work in schools and colleges, which I will really enjoy.

We have clear structure and processes to work with as Business Doctors and a variety of effective tools to deploy within our clients' businesses. We have vast experience at our disposal and we have so far supported over ten thousand businesses in the UK. We provide affordable support to help business owners make the right choices for growth. Practice, dedication and experience have made us experts in our field, but what particularly attracted me to Business Doctors was their down-to-earth approach. We don't just coach; we get on the pitch.

For me though, it still comes down to those two key building blocks from my Procter & Gamble days: *Leading people and building business.*

What I always enjoyed and what helped to keep me motivated through my sales and marketing career was the variety in my responsibilities. Selling, planning, negotiation, analysis, coaching, training, recruiting— mine was never a nine-to-five or desk-bound role. However, around forty thousand miles of driving, twenty to twenty-five long train journeys and a dozen or so flights every year did take its toll and one benefit of Covid-19 is the emergence of Zoom, Teams and so on as viable alternatives to some of that travel!

Back to Business Doctors and that variety of responsibilities and different challenges is still very much there and, if anything, is even greater.

Across those two building blocks we get involved in all of the following (and even more) with our clients:

Building Business	**Leading People & Culture**
• Strategic planning	• Organisation design
• Sales management	• Staff engagement
• Marketing and communication	• People and performance management
• Forecasting and cash flow	• Recruitment and psychometric assessment
• Business performance management	• Maximising performance though training and development
• Finding funding and financial support	• Implementation of strategy and interim support
• Business valuations and exit plans	• 'Director on Demand' service
• Local business community support through Chambers of Commerce	

In terms of business valuations and exit plans we work with the Value Builder System founded by John Warrillow from Toronto. John is an accomplished author of many business books including *The Automatic Customer, Built to Sell* and *The Art of Selling Your Business*. The Value Builder System is a powerful tool that analyses a business across a number of criteria to estimate its value and identify areas that can be developed to increase that value over time. Comparative data from over fifty thousand other businesses are used as benchmarks.

Whether business owners are thinking of a major change or would just like a base-point valuation, Value Builder provides simple and highly effective analysis.

In closing, I'd like to say good luck to all my readers in your careers and with your business ventures. I hope by reading this you have gained some simple ideas and suggestions for supporting your personal development and enhancing your leadership, based on the successes and mistakes of myself and others. I also hope that some of the stories shared have raised a smile, as we all need a bit of levity in our lives.

And please remember:

For your business to prosper,

Contact Steve, the Business Doctor!

PICTURES SAY A THOUSAND WORDS

Early Days

I never met my paternal grandfather, Evander Jackson Tames as he died before I was born. He was apparently an interesting character who became bitter and resentful of the society and leaders who had taken the country into the appalling carnage of World War One. He was a confirmed atheist and associate of the renowned socialist and future Labour MP for Liverpool Exchange, Bessie Braddock. They were both involved in the Liverpool branch of the Communist Party of Great Britain in the 1920s. I have a few of my grandfather's possessions, including a first edition printing of Erich Maria Remarque's anti-war novel *All Quiet on the Western Front* and his air raid warden whistle from World War Two. I also have a little book belonging to my mother in which he wrote important and enduring advice in 1951 when she was just nine years old.

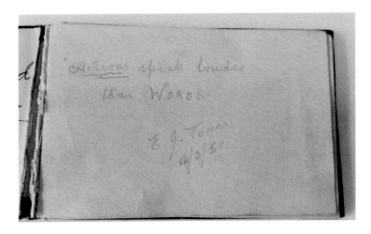

His actions certainly spoke louder than his words. He walked the talk by not walking. Being atheist, he would not go into the church for my mother and father's wedding, only joining them later for the reception!

My first real leadership role was captaining my primary school football team. I am holding the ball and you can see that we won a few trophies.

University of Sheffield 1987-90

With my mum the morning I departed for Sheffield University. Unfortunately, she never got to see me graduate.

I loved my time at university despite losing my mum in my second year. I was elected president of Sorby Hall (of residence) Junior Common Room, which set me off on my career path and leadership journey. I only appreciated the true impact of my mum's passing in later years. I was beyond childhood but a long way off being a mature adult at that point. I did some stupid things over the next few years, nothing serious, but things I wish I could change now.

Each year we had a hall photograph taken. It was the old style, slow exposure panoramic photo and if quick enough, someone could start on the left, run around the back and appear again on the right-hand side! On the second of the three sections from 1988 is a future European Zone President of Anheuser-Busch InBev and at the time of writing the current MD of Weetabix.

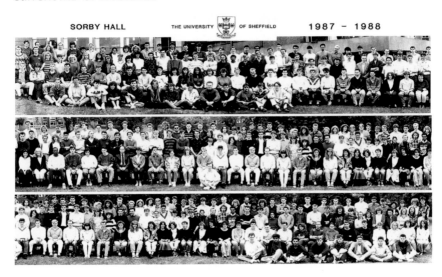

The outgoing hall president Joe McCarthy is seated central next to the hall warden who is wearing a tie, and I'm over on the right in the final section below, about twelve in on the third row up.

Below is a photo of Joe and me at the formal dinner to hand over the presidency. In some ways we had little in common but became good friends. Joe was a great support when I lost my mum and pushed me hard to pass my exams and learn from his own experience of having to re-sit exams over the previous summer.

He was an amazing character and would surely have achieved incredible things in his life if it had not been cruelly cut short at the Hillsborough tragedy.

You'll Never Walk Alone, Joe.

Procter & Gamble 1990-99

It was holding student office that brought me to the attention of Procter & Gamble and they invited me to attend their sales management vacation course at the end of 1989. It ran for three days at the Runnymede Hotel in Surrey and was the first time I had ever stayed in a hotel. I was central in the back row. Sales VP John Millen occupied the central position. He was a true gentleman and a great leader who offered me the chance to return to Procter & Gamble if my move to Kellogg's did not work out.

Note they were still using the moon and thirteen stars symbol—if there were any satanic orgies, I was not invited. I returned as a trainer on the course several years later.

I was offered a job as account executive in sales, providing I passed my degree. Thirteen thousand, four hundred pounds a year with a company car and training from one of the original blue-chip companies. How could I resist?

My dad worked as a forklift truck driver on a three-shift system at Ford's Halewood car factory for over thirty years. The workforce in the seventies and eighties were notoriously militant and it sometimes seemed like they were on strike more than they worked! My parents wanted much better for their children. I worked as a summer intern in HR at the plant in 1989. The picture overleaf is from a twenty-five years' of service celebratory lunch for my dad (right).

Steven J. Smith

The training was first class. Two courses in one month!

Certificate of Accomplishment

This certifies that

Steven Smith

has participated in
and successfully completed

Interpersonal Managing Skills

1.Feb 91   Bian h Lad   R.H.G.Gray
Date   Administrator

C.G. 19m r
Managing Director

Learning
INTERNATIONAL

Total Quality Management

THIS CERTIFICATE IS AWARDED TO

Steve Smith

in recognition of completion of

IMPLEMENTING TOTAL QUALITY-I

J. E. Pepper, President

John O'Keeffe

Presented by

13th February 1991
Date

I was invited to return to Sheffield University for a week, as a young manager, helping undergraduates on a career development course (fourth from left).

At my desk in Procter & Gamble's Harrogate office in 1994, looking a bit worse for wear. Check out the size of that monitor and desktop computer!

I did not really enjoy my time in head office in Gosforth. The role was great experience and I worked with some incredibly talented people, but it was all a bit too formal for me. At the management meeting below in November 1995, only Ricky Reed at the front looks genuinely happy.

After Gosforth, I moved to Procter & Gamble's health & beauty care (HABC) division where the culture was a lot more relaxed. Below was a team-building event at a sales meeting; we did not dress like that!

My first real team—the Wild Geese of Skelmersdale. The UK general manager, Mohan, had heard good things about the culture we had developed and paid a visit. His replacement 'talked the talk' but did not walk it from my experience. Margaret next to me was originally the team PA. We developed her role into an office manager.

My Asda ABCD Award. They may well have become more of a gimmick over time, however, this is an authentic early edition signed by Allan Leighton CEO and sent direct to John Millen, Procter & Gamble's sales vice president. I've kept it for over twenty years and am proud of it!

AWARD

"Above and Beyond the Call of Duty"

This certifies that

Steve Smith

has received this award for actions truly Above and Beyond the Call of Duty.

ALLAN LEIGHTON
Chief Executive

A European sales college training course in 1998 where I was a moderator (back row second left) supporting the course leader (first left) Kevin Hawkins. Kevin was my manager for my national account role on Kwik Save and had a discerning taste for dessert!

I enjoyed the European training and meeting colleagues from various countries. This was still relatively soon after the fall of the Berlin Wall and the opening of Eastern Europe's economies.

Kellogg's 1999-04

Dinner (tea) one evening on my first Kellogg's sales and marketing conference in January 2000 in Puerto Banus. As part of the leadership group, I was in Spain for nearly a week. The previous year, the conference had been at Slaley Hall, Northumberland. It was dark, cold and rained incessantly. The new MD who'd just joined from Australia was horrified. 'F**k that, we're goin' somewhere sunny next year!' was his frequently repeated quote.

The England 1966 World Cup winners in 2002, with myself next to the late, great Alan Ball on the right. We had TV and press coverage lined up to promote Kellogg's involvement with the event until Roy Keane intervened! Still, a great night was had by all. Alan, June from the Coop, and myself were the last ones standing in the hotel afterwards. I helped Alan back to his room at about 4am! One of the most enjoyable evenings of my entire career.

The free toys in boxes of cereal were a key part of growing up in the seventies and eighties, though the comparison with the more expensive toys McDonald's provided with Happy Meals became a significant challenge.

I had loads of fun working with Kellogg's kids' brands, providing fact-filled growth charts and free 'foot-bowls' with in-store purchases. That particular execution was repeated several times after I had departed and there must still be thousands in kitchen cupboards across the UK. For one project, variety pack packaging became trucks, buses and even Santa's sleigh. Another promotion delivered a free t-shirt. Kellogg's also supported some fabulous movie launches through partnerships with Disney and Warner Brothers.

AG Barr 2004-19

R & R's more common meeting as we launched Rockstar in 2007. Sir Anwar Pervez, Chairman of Bestway Group, is central. We gave customers a real taste of Las Vegas with a helicopter trip to the Grand Canyon and ringside seats for the Ricky Hatton versus Floyd Mayweather fight.

Ringside with Lennox Lewis. I also shook hands with Brad Pitt—Angelina Jolie looking on, somewhat bemused. To be fair, a day at work doesn't really get much better than this.

Thank you, Rockstar, thank you, AG Barr!

With the Bestway Incentive winners studying the energy drinks' market in Las Vegas 2016. I am third from right, Martin Race then Bestway's MD is third from left.

Presenting the Rockstar brand to customers back in Glasgow—trying to look cool and failing!!

Talking football with the Everton manager David Moyes at the Scottish Football League Awards in 2010. It was fascinating to hear about the inner workings of football and discuss the importance of IRN-BRU in Scotland.

Barr participated in several Charity Celebrity Football Tournaments organised by the grocery retailers. Great fun, a good chance to get to know senior figures in the customers and an opportunity to test yourself against ex-pros. We got to the final one year, but never quite got our hands on a trophy.

Tesco Charity 5-a-side Football Legends Tournament
10th March 2011

AG Barr had a very close relationship with the Prince and Princess of Wales Hospice in Glasgow. As well as accepting one of their charity places for the 2008 London Marathon (I raised four thousand, five hundred pounds with some very generous donations, particularly from customers) the team raised thousands for the hospice's 'Brick by Brick' appeal to help fund the move to new premises. Each year we sponsored the hospice's main fundraising event, the Sportsman's Dinner.

In the picture above are Jan Molby (former Liverpool footballer), Sean Styles (comedian), Fergus Slattery and Martin Bayfield (Ireland/England and Lions rugby union internationals respectively). On other occasions I got to meet my own childhood football heroes Duncan MacKenzie and Johan Cruyff, Manchester United stars Gary Neville and Peter Schmeichal, boxing legend Joe Calzaghe and tennis ace Greg Rusedski—plus many others. An absolute privilege to be on the top table with such achievers.

When IRN-BRU invested in becoming the official soft drink of the Super League we were determined to get involved with the sport and not just be a passive sponsor. We held our sales meetings at Rugby League stadiums such as St Helens, Wigan and at Warrington, pictured in 2011.

To help the sales team relate to the sport, I invited the late Steve Prescott MBE (front centre with myself to the left) to share his story about success on the field and fighting a rare form of stomach cancer off it. His incredible endurance feats during fundraising whilst battling the debilitating disease were an inspiration. This was one of his first public speaking engagements and he admitted to a fair degree of nerves. He was asked about this by one of the audience members who wondered how he could perform so well in front of a hundred thousand people in a Challenge Cup Final at Wembley yet be nervous talking in front of our group. Steve's answer illustrates the power of teamwork and interdependency—'I had twelve mates on the pitch supporting me at Wembley, here I'm on my own.'

We were proud to support the Steve Prescott Foundation in several fundraising events.

I am partnering ex-Premier League referee Chris Foy in the dragon boat with Steve behind us.

With my son and guests on the pitch at St Helen's Rugby League Club after sponsoring a game.

One of the high points of 2020 was when the Saints edged out fierce rivals Wigan at the end of the Super League Grand Final. The word 'derby' to describe sports events between near neighbours originated from this fixture. These historical combatants fought out a truly titanic struggle, only decided by the last play of the game. No one deserved to lose and despite my St Helens' allegiance I did genuinely feel for Wigan and their supporters.

What also stood out was the humility and sportsmanship of the Wigan captain Sean O'Loughlin. In the final game of a long and illustrious career, his grace and magnanimity in defeat was something you rarely see in other sports.

Celebrating two of our many successes in the Bestway Awards, firstly with Guy Gissing and Vinnie Liddar in 2012—they did an incredible job developing our relevance and relationship with one of the UK's largest wholesalers. As a point of principle, I always insisted that Vinnie or Guy receive the award; they were the ones who earned them.

In 2013, Guy and Vinnie are joined by Steve Brooks (second left, who ran the regional sales team), Steven, Deryn and Stevie. Those four had over one hundred years AG Barr service among them and pioneered a new form of artwork by building incredible displays in UK cash & carries. Below is the Dubai Palm, re-created in Rubicon and KA drinks.

Presenting to AG Barr's Middlebrook office.

Middlebrook was a great place to work, full of life, with wonderful friendly colleagues and described by one person as a 'sanctuary'. We obtained Investors in People (IIP) silver status and always got the highest site scores in AG Barr's employee engagement survey.

Karen is central on the front row and was a great support. Her role developed from sales secretarial supervisor, up to office manager leading the team.

Michelle from the operations team later replied to one of my posts on LinkedIn, writing: 'You are an inspiration. Your kind, encouraging and positive attitude and behaviour will stay with me. You touched peoples' lives and I don't think you know what a lasting impression you made.'

To have someone who did not even report to you summarise your career with such words is simply priceless.

Winter Hill and Rivington Pike dominate the landscape close to the Middlebrook office. I would often run up there after work to reflect and switch off on the way back down.

There were some great characters and lovely people up in Scotland but the atmosphere at Barr head office in Cumbernauld was a little quiet and library-like. We were always encouraged to let our hair down and have fun at the annual company conference though! Over the years, I presented dressed as a Spartan hoplite, Spitfire pilot, Adam Ant and wearing Bavarian lederhosen.

The last meeting with my AG Barr team. Jonathan, the commercial director is next to me and 'Wee Ian' is behind. Ian led the team in Scotland to numerous awards and was one of the great characters I met during my career. He is the type of person you would always want next to you in the trenches, or 'shield wall', given his love of Bernard Cornwell novels.

I had developed a close relationship with one of our customers, the Café on the Pier at Lytham St Anne's. They gave us exclusive use of their facilities for the evening and looked after us very, very well! Bad heads the next day.

AG Barr plc's share price during the time I was there. I left in July 2019. The price dropped significantly. I am just saying… There was obviously far more to it than that!

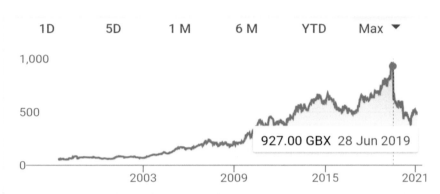

ACKNOWLEDGEMENTS

I have worked with so many people over the course of my career that I have chosen to just pick out a few key names who had a positive impact. There are many, many others who I have looked at with respect and followed their example, then also those whose *modus operandi* I have questioned and decided to handle situations in what I considered a better way. Either way, major learnings were taken from both and I am grateful. There are many incredibly gifted people I've referenced who can explain their work far better. With the glories of Google, a greater understanding of any subject is rarely more than a few clicks away.

At the University of Sheffield, I enjoyed the marketing lectures by Everett M Jacobs and in later life fully appreciated the lessons in maturity provided by Dr David E Bland OBE. I have also never forgotten Anthony Levi. If he hadn't driven a Ford Transit Minibus over the A57 Snake Pass in the early hours of a wet January morning, I'd never have seen my mum before she died. I am eternally grateful to Anthony.

Joining Procter & Gamble was crucial to how I developed. I was recruited by Steve Gray, and then Kevin C Hawkins supplied excellent guidance and the idea behind this story a long time ago. John Forsyth showed a willingness to think differently and challenge the status quo, whilst Richard C H Reed is a quintessential English gentleman who always cared for his people and finds time, even now, to provide help and support.

At Kellogg's, Stephen Twaddell recruited me to be part of his crusade to modernise the sales function. The training he commissioned has helped me ever since by introducing the inspirational thinking of Helen-Jane Nelson of Cecara Consulting. Dan Beck reported to me in Kellogg's and eventually followed me to AG Barr where he provided friendship, support, and the benefit of his unique skillset.

I spent fifteen years with AG Barr working directly for commercial director Jonathan D Kemp, one of the brightest people I ever worked with. He was previously my friend at Procter & Gamble (despite inheriting the MBW project from me!). We made a great partnership, with a complimentary blend of the 3E's. Finance director Stuart Lorimer shared kind and encouraging words when I was leaving. Karen Sharples, originally my PA and then promoted to office manager was an absolute pleasure to work with and a key confidante. Karen's team were great fun, and we had some hilarious moments in the Middlebrook office.

Others who have provided support in various ways include Kevin and Rosemary Taylor from Vivvid, Martin Race, former MD of Bestway, Miles Mandelson, my next-door neighbour, my brother Paul (who offered reassurance in my darker days), and Matt Keefe who provided valuable feedback on early versions. Bill Byrne the MD of Churchill Search & Selection has been a great friend and sounding board for twenty-five years with Matt Levington, Rod Davies and Kevin 'Obi-wan' Cook of Business Doctors now fulfilling that role. Andrew Selley, CEO of Bidcorp, is a leader who impressed me greatly in his role as chairman of the Federation of Wholesale Distributors. Andrew introduced me to the wonderful Denise Roberts of The Editor's Chair who made Baked Alaska become a reality.

Alan McKie of Halton Chamber has offered me loads of encouragement, whilst John Tabern, CEO of The Standing Tall Foundation and chairman of St Helens Town Deal Board is someone I've worked with on various projects over the years. I've been warmly welcomed into the local business community and appreciate the help given by the likes of Lisa McAllister, Jayne Shufflebotham, Geoff Bates' team at St Helens Chamber and Jim Toohey who I first met over thirty years ago when he was a store manager with Morrisons.

Colin Parry OBE is someone I have admired from afar for a long, long time and it was a pleasure meeting him in 2019 for coaching and support. To me, he defines the word dignity. It was a genuine honour when he agreed to write a foreword.

Last, but certainly not least, is my wife Gillian who nursed me through my stroke recovery and has always had more confidence in my abilities than I have had myself. I would never have completed this without her love, positivity, and encouragement.

'Me, we.'

Muhammed Ali